More JEWISH *Culture & Customs*

More JEWISH *Culture & Customs*

A Sampler of Jewish Life

by Steve Herzig

The Friends of Israel Gospel Ministry, Inc.
P. O. Box 908, Bellmawr, NJ 08099

More JEWISH CULTURE & CUSTOMS
A Sampler of Jewish Life

Steve Herzig

Copyright © 2004 by The Friends of Israel Gospel Ministry, Inc.
Bellmawr, New Jersey 08099

Unless otherwise noted, all Scripture is quoted from *The New Scofield Study Bible*, Authorized King James Version, Oxford University Press, Inc., 1967.

Printed in the United States of America
Library of Congress Catalog Card Number: 2004106162
ISBN 0-915540-44-4

INSIDE PHOTOGRAPHS: Cathy Raff, p. 94, copyright © Cathy Raff; Hanan Isacar, p. 122, copyright © Hanan Isacar

Cover by Waveline Direct, Mechanicsburg, PA.

Visit our Web site at *www.foi.org*.

TABLE OF CONTENTS

DEDICATION 7

FOREWORD 9

THE PALE OF SETTLEMENT 11

THE PIONEERING SPIRIT 15

RETURNING TO THE LAND 21

LOST HOPE RECLAIMED 27

THE MAN WHO BROUGHT HEBREW BACK TO THE LAND . . .33

THE FIRST LINE OF DEFENSE 39

ARE THERE HORNS UNDER THAT HAT?
MYTHS ABOUT THE JEWISH PEOPLE 47

IS THE NEW TESTAMENT ANTI-SEMITIC 55

WHO KILLED JESUS? 63

JEWISH HUMOR 67

JEWISH MUSIC 73

FROM BADGE TO BANNER 85

BAPTISM OR MIKVEH? 89

TRY IT—YOU'LL LIKE IT! 95

WHAT'S IN A NAME? 101

SO, WHAT EXACTLY IS THAT? 105

A DAY FOR REMEMBERING YOM HASHOAH 111

THE CALL OF THE SHOFAR 117

GIVING AND RECEIVING THE BLESSING 123

ALIYAH FOR THE PEOPLE OF THE BOOK 127

BLESSINGS ON YOUR HEAD 133

JUDAISM VS. JEWISHNESS 139

CHOSEN? FOR WHAT? 145

WHEN YOU'RE DEAD, YOU'RE DEAD 151

PONDERING THE QUESTION OF EVIL 157

TIKKUN OLAM 163

THE TATTOO IS TABOO 169

ORGANIZED FOR SERVICE 173

WORKMEN'S CIRCLE 179

POLITICS & POLITICIANS 185

AKIVA: ASCENSION TO PROMINENCE 191

WANTING TO BE A SOMEBODY .197

PLAY BALL 201

ENDNOTES 207

DEDICATION

To David and Beverly Levy
Their devotion to Christ and love for God's Chosen People has served as a constant example to me. Early in my ministry they challenged me to step out in faith in various life situations. They never failed to be available as sounding boards for even my craziest ideas. Always they listened. Whatever positive ministry the Lord has been pleased to provide, none of it would be possible without them. I thank them with all my heart.

FOREWORD

THOUSANDS OF READERS WERE INSPIRED and instructed by Steve Herzig's first volume of *Jewish Culture & Customs*, a sampler of Jewish life. At the close of his introduction to that book, Steve promised, "As the Lord enables, it is my desire to follow this with another volume." Now his desire has come to fruition, and we are delighted to introduce volume II, *More Jewish Culture & Customs*. And it comes none too soon. Requests for more insights into the lives and customs of the Jewish people have come to us from across North America.

Steve, who grew up as an Orthodox Jew, has clearly stated his motive in writing on the subject. Many Jewish people, he said, are uninformed about the customs and culture of their own people. And, that being the case, he said, "imagine the lack of understanding that exists in the Gentile community. This void is of little concern to most Gentiles, but there is one segment of the community that does care a great deal: the true Christians, born-again and Bible-believing. They consider themselves people of God and have a tremendous love for the Jewish people.

"The reason for this is simple. Jesus the Messiah was born a Jew in Israel, the land God promised to His people. His followers were all Jews who practiced their faith. Anyone who holds the Scriptures to be the Word of God will desire a better understanding of the people He chose and called 'the apple of his eye'" (Zech. 2:8).

More Jewish Culture & Customs is a captivating and sometimes bittersweet excursion into the history and richness of Jewish life. I'm sure you will be touched, amused, uplifted, inspired, and instructed as you read this book. Only one word of warning: It will certainly leave you wanting more. Perhaps we should nudge Steve in that direction in the not-too-distant future!

Elwood McQuaid
Editor-in-Chief

The Statue of Liberty in New York Harbor with a map of the Pale of Settlement in the background.

THE PALE OF SETTLEMENT

MANY YEARS AGO A BOOK AND THEN a television miniseries captured our attention. The story was *Roots*, and in it the author traced his family's history all the way back to Africa.

An understanding of our family background—how our ancestors lived and how they came to the United States from their countries of origin—satisfies a curiosity in many of us. For me and other Jewish people with Eastern European ancestry, tracing our roots can be a frustrating task. My parents told me that my grandparents arrived in the United States through the dreaded Ellis Island around 1905. That was the easy part of answering my queries. The hard part came when they tried to tell me the country they came from. There were several possible answers—Russia, Austria, Hungary, Poland. My parents were never sure because they said the borders of the countries kept shifting. Then, in Hebrew school, I heard the term *the Pale* for the first time. Understanding this term and this place finally helped clear up my vagueness as to my ancestors' origins.

This place of changing boundaries was called *the Pale of Settlement*, a term coined during the reign of Czar Nicholas I of Russia. By 1835, he was forced to deal with a large and unwanted Jewish population that had come under his rule when Russia annexed Poland in 1772. The Pale was a restricted region, yet it possessed no official borders. It covered an area from the Baltic Sea to the Black Sea, and at its peak its population swelled to nearly five million Jewish people. Many people groups from such nations as Ukraine, Belorussia, Lithuania, and Poland lived in the Pale. It was established by the Russians to prevent the Jewish population from mingling with Russians. The Pale also made it possible to insure a Gentile majority in most places. Exceptions did occur in such cities as Minsk, Warsaw, and Odessa.

Force was often used to remove Jews living outside the Pale. The message was clear: No Jews were allowed outside the Pale. This policy caused incredible economic hardship. Limited to a primarily agricultural economy and yet forbidden by law to own their own land, the Jewish people became the tailors, bakers, peddlers, and small store owners. This meant that what little work there was in the Pale had to be shared among many. Hunger, even starvation, was all too common.

A goal of all the Russian czars was to assimilate as many Jewish people as possible. One czarist advisor suggested that one third should be starved to death, one third driven from the country, and one third baptized. One way to accomplish that objective was through the conscription of men into the Russian army. Gentiles had to serve from the age of eighteen for a term of twenty-five years. Jewish men had to serve six years longer, beginning at the age of twelve. It was believed that by preventing bar mitzvah and contact with their parents during their teen years, the young men would be "Russianized." If the required monthly quota of recruits was not met, "snatchers" would come and literally take young Jewish men off the streets. It was not uncommon to hear the shriek, "Snatchers are coming! Snatchers are coming!" Naturally, this brought sheer terror to the mothers of the communities. Many young boys were snatched right out of their mothers' arms.

An even worse problem subsequently arose, particularly in the l9th century. Cities large and small were raided, burned, and plundered. The authorities did nothing to stop the carnage and, in fact, encouraged it. In 1903 the violence reached its peak in Kishineff, when a riotous mob killed thousands of Jews, including scores of little children. The rest of the world condemned this barbarism. President Roosevelt sent an official protest to the czar to stop the horrible pogroms.

It was during this time that Jews in record numbers began their great migration to what many called in Yiddish the *Goldenah Medina*, the *Golden Land*—the United States of America. As they entered New York Harbor, their first sight was of Lady Liberty welcoming the weary travelers. "Give me your tired, your poor, your huddled masses yearning to breathe free, the wretched refuse of your teeming shores. Send these, the homeless, tempest tossed, to me. I lift my lamp beside the golden door." These words, inscribed on the Statue of Liberty, were written by a Jewess, Emma Lazarus, whose heart had been touched by the plight of this persecuted people. Their safe arrival on our shores inspired her poem, *The New Colossus*.

In the years between 1881 and 1917, well over two million tired, poor, homeless, tempest-tossed Jews—the largest influx in American history—scrounged and saved to come to America because they yearned to breathe free. By God's grace, my four grandparents were among them.

*The author's grandparents
Lena and Markus Wulkan in 1907.*

*The author's grandparents
Ida and Sam Herzig in 1914.*

THE PIONEERING SPIRIT

THE PIONEERING SPIRIT HAS ALWAYS captivated me. Remnants of wagon trails can still be seen in various Western states. The courage and tenacity displayed by those trailblazers are lessons for all of us. Yet, as much as I admire those brave Americans who ventured West, it boggles my mind to think of those who traveled, not across our country, but across the sea!

My grandparents left the Pale of Settlement as teenagers— a tiny part of the largest group of immigrants in U.S. history. More than two million Jewish people, primarily from Eastern Europe, sought refuge in the *Goldenah Medina* during that time. One of the greatest Yiddish writers of all time, Sholom Aleichem, once said, "On the train to the border [to take the ship to America] when we hear the word 'America,' we rejoice. 'So you are going to New York!' 'We are going to Philadelphia.' 'What is Philadelphia?' 'A town like New York.'"

What actually happened to all of those immigrant people? Where did they go? What did they do? How did they live?

From today's perspective, we may have a somewhat romantic view of the monumental voyage made by our forebears. In reality, it was a dangerous and frightening journey made by many adventurous and courageous people. Most of the Jewish immigrants arrived from Europe through Ellis Island, a little piece of land located in New York Harbor, about a mile southwest of Manhattan. Now a museum, it stands as a testament to the twelve million people who were processed there over a sixty-year period.

Processing upon arrival often took several days. The most dreaded aspect of the ordeal was the eye exam. Inspectors checked the eyes for a disease called trachoma, a form of conjunctivitis. Failing this test meant immediate return to Europe. The thought of being sent back to the pogroms was horrifying. Ellis Island came to be known as the *Isle of Tears* because of the heart-wrenching situations that caused such dreaded news. Many who failed the exam or did not have the necessary documentation tried to escape by jumping into the harbor and swimming to New York. Many suicides were attempted, and some were successful. If papers were approved and physicals were passed, the new arrivals could set foot—finally and legally—in America.

Settling into American life usually meant finding your way to the Lower East Side of the borough of Manhattan. Bordering the Brooklyn Bridge on the south, 14th Street on the north, Broadway on the west, and the East River on the east, this environment was a long way from the *shtetls* (small towns or villages) left behind. Everything was different—language, population density, means of transportation, food, clothing. One new immigrant wrote, "I'd never had ice cream before. It was new to me in America. We walked and ate. When we passed girls, my brothers wanted to give them a taste of our ice cream. The girls refused. I felt as if on coals. No word could I think of but 'greenhorn.'"[1] Another immigrant commented on a woman chewing gum as "making a queer motion with the muscles of her mouth." He wondered what kind of mouth disease she had.

Often one family member would come first, then work and save to finance the trip for the rest of the family. Needless to say, this created great hardship; at times the task was impossible. Coming to the aid of some of these unfortunates were philanthropic organizations, which had been started by wealthy benefactors—immigrants themselves who had prospered in this new land and desired to help their people. *Landmanschaften* (Jewish brotherhood lodges) were also formed to help minister to these new arrivals. The *landsman* was always there to try to help. The large influx of immigrants corresponded to a time of U.S. industrial expansion. Jobs were plentiful—but very low paying. A phenomenon called the *sweatshop* emerged. Lowly workers toiled under terrible conditions for fourteen to sixteen hours a day, earning $4 to $8 a week. "Sweatshop poets" emerged to elucidate their feelings:

> I work, and I work, without
> rhyme, without reason—
>   produce, and produce, and
> produce without end.
>   For what? And for whom?
> I don't know, I don't wonder
>   —since when can a whirling
> machine comprehend?
>
>   No feelings, no thoughts, not
> the least understanding;
>   this bitter, this murderous
> drudgery drains
>   the noblest, the finest,
> the best and the richest,
>   the deepest, the highest that
> living contains.[2]

This was particularly true in the garment industry, which employed many Jewish workers. Terrible working conditions fostered disease and danger, many factories being nothing more than firetraps and other types of disasters waiting to happen. The most infamous tragedy was the Triangle Shirtwaist Factory disaster in 1911, in which fire swept through a building where the doors had been locked to keep the workers from getting out. One hundred and forty-six people died in that fire.

Tuberculosis also was a common occurrence, resulting from the pace of the work and the conditions endured.

Some Jewish people traveled south and west to other urban areas to be near families or hoping for better opportunities. All four of my grandparents ventured to Cleveland, Ohio. My father's mother worked in a cigar factory for $5 a week, while my grandfather used his skill as a tailor to do piecework. Later he parlayed that skill to open his own dry-cleaning store. It was through the Jewish immigrants from Russia that labor was organized to fight the poor conditions and eventually to form the Amalgamated Clothing Workers of America and the International Ladies Garment Workers Union, which helped not only the Jewish labor force, but all laborers.

Life was not all misery, however. America benefited from the presence of these newcomers, who usually tried to improve whatever situation they found themselves in. Yiddish newspapers, most notably *The Jewish Daily Forward*, provided world news and articles on religion, fashion, poetry, current events, and trends. One such trend that began during this period, as reported in *The Forward*, was expressed in a new Yiddish word, *oysesn*, or *eating out*—not at the home of a relative or a friend, but in an actual restaurant. This was something unheard of in the old country. The newspaper also offered the *Bintel Brief*—letters to the editor—which gave tremendous insight into the lives of the immigrants. Yiddish theater provided entertainment, a temporary respite from the hardships of daily life.

At the height of this immigration came the rise of the resorts. Hotels located in the Catskill Mountains in upstate New York offered clean air and kosher meals, as well as the joy of getting out of the hot, muggy city. It was from the dinner fare served to the Jewish clientele that these resorts came to be known as the

Borscht Belt. Years later the pattern of these entertainment spas was modeled in Miami Beach, Florida.

Millions of Jewish people, myself included, thank our sovereign God for bringing our relatives to America's shores. Here my people were given opportunities to make a new life for themselves—and here many have been given the opportunity to receive eternal life.

RETURNING TO THE LAND

WANTED
People Interested in Adventure
NEEDED
Desire to work hard in hostile
environment with few resources
REMUNERATION
None

NOT EVERYONE WHO EMIGRATED CAME to America. Many Jewish people decided to return to the land of their forefathers—*Eretz Yisrael*—the land of Israel. After the turn of the twentieth century, forty thousand Jewish people made *aliya* (immigration to Israel), knowing they had no more to gain than the promise of the fictitious ad above. Most of these brave adventurers were Eastern Europeans, descendants of the *Diaspora*, the Jewish community that has been scattered throughout the world since the Roman invasion of Jerusalem in A.D. 70.

What would compel entire families to make such a difficult move back to the land of their ancestors? What possible advantage could there be in going to a place that offered virtually nothing but backbreaking work?

First, these people sought peace. In oppressive, Czarist Russia in particular, the Jewish people were being murdered en masse in pogroms, the result of blatant anti-Semitism. Second, they sought independence. For centuries, Jews had been denied the privilege of owning land and were beholden to their Gentile landowners. Third, the time was right. The first Zionist Congress, held in Basle, Switzerland, in 1897, was energizing the Jewish people in the Diaspora with a Zionistic fervor that gave these idealistic pioneers the hope they needed to chase their dreams.

Although they tended toward socialistic ideas, they were still very much Jewish. Zionism's goal was to "establish for the Jewish people a publicly and legally assured home in Palestine."[1] It was a movement that fueled real hope that some-day a place would exist on this planet where being Jewish would not be a crime.

These young pioneers highly esteemed hard physical labor and considered it a blessing, not a burden, to reclaim the malaria-infested swamps and barren desert of Israel through the sweat of their brows. Working the sun-scorched soil of their ancestors with their own hands became a dream come true. Their immigration ushered in the dawn of a new movement. These are the tireless men and women who established the *kibbutz* (collective or communal community) forty years before the birth of the modern State of Israel.

From the beginning, the operating principle has been "from each according to his ability, to each according to his needs."[2]

These communities even today are comprised of people who genuinely want to live there. They are free to leave whenever they wish, and they govern themselves through democratic rule. The membership meets regularly, affording opportunity to register opinions and/or grievances. All major decisions are made by the membership (*chaverim*), each person possessing one vote. The individual owns nothing; the *kibbutz* owns everything. The collective decides and provides for all individual needs. Cars, clothes, food, health care, education—every physical need is provided. The community exists for the benefit of its members. The first *kibbutzniks* (individual members) faced an enormous task. The great majority had no agricultural experience and possessed few resources. They were pioneers in a land that had lain desolate for years and was subject to drought as well as to raids by nearby enemies.

It was as in the days of Nehemiah, that "half of my servants wrought in the work, and the other half of them held the spears, the shields, and the bows, and the coats of mail" (Neh. 4:16). Thus it was common for a *kibbutznik* to be working in the field with hoe or shovel and a rifle slung over his shoulder. Before 1948 and the War of Independence, *kibbutzim* were used to train Jews to defend themselves against terrorism, a constant intruder. Each member of each *kibbutz* has always understood the need to be completely self-sufficient. Since most *kibbutzim* were located near borders and served as defense fortifications, every *kibbutznik* knew that each conflict was a fight to protect not just the homeland but also his own home. It is not surprising, therefore, that a large percentage of Israel's military officers have come from *kibbutzim*.

Kibbutzniks also take great pride in their country, and a number have become dedicated civil servants. David Ben-Gurion, the first prime minister of the State of Israel, was himself a *kibbutznik*. He returned to his *kibbutz* in the Negev after retiring from public life in 1963.

In addition to contributing to the defense of their country, *kibbutzim* have helped immigration. Many provide *ulpan*, a five-month, intensive Hebrew-language study course for new immigrants.

All responsibilities in *kibbutz* life are shared equally between men and women who hold jobs on a rotating basis, including supervisory positions. The *kibbutz* owns all the land, all the equipment, all the homes. Food also is produced on the *kibbutz*. Crops vary but include oranges, lemons, artichokes, bananas, dates, olives, apples, cotton, tomatoes, peanuts, and walnuts. *Kibbutzniks* also raise livestock, such as cows, chickens, turkeys, and even fish. Today many *kibbutzim* sustain a variety of manufacturing facilities in light industry. Meals are prepared by *kibbutz* members, most of whom dine in the community dining room. In the early years, children were reared in community nurseries, visiting their parents only once a week. In many *kibbutzim* today, this system has changed. Children sleep in the homes of their parents, often enjoying some of their meals together.

The first *kibbutz*, Degenyah (God's wheat), was established in 1909. Its 750 acres are located on the southern tip of Lake Kinneret (Sea of Galilee). It began with just ten men and two women, and the average age was twenty. The land was purchased by an agency of the World Zionist Organization called The Jewish National Fund (JNF), or *Keren Kayemet L' Yisrael*. This organization was founded for the purpose of purchasing land for the Jewish people. Its Hebrew name is derived from a Talmudic dictum about good deeds, "the fruits of which a man enjoys in this world while the capital abides [*ha-keren kayemet*] for him in the world to come" (pe'ah 1:1).[3]

Before the Holy Land had become the State of Israel, JNF purchased thousands of acres from absentee Arab owners who regarded it as useless. At first, land acquisition was JNF's chief purpose. Once Israel became a nation, JNF shifted its purpose from acquiring land to developing it. Many people, including evangelical Christians, assist the JNF even today in forestation programs. The Friends of Israel Forest located outside Jerusalem was established under the authority of the JNF. Millions of trees have been planted there. JNF also has been involved in irrigation projects, flood control, and establishing campgrounds and picnic facilities.

Today approximately 275 *kibbutzim* exist around the country. Yet many people are surprised to learn that only 120,000 or so *kibbutzniks*, or 2.3 percent of Israel's population, actually live on a *kibbutz*. Most of today's Israelis would say it is not a lifestyle they would choose. When young *kibbutzniks* return from their required time in military service, they must choose whether to become members of the *kibbutz* or leave. Only about 40 percent stay.

Yet, despite their small numbers, *kibbutzim* produce a third of all Israeli agricultural products and nearly 10 percent of all goods manufactured in the country. Combined, these constitute 12 percent of the gross national product. *Kibbutzim* are key to the country's ability to introduce young people to the land. Jewish youth groups, colleges, and synagogues send their young people to experience Israel through a *kibbutz*. Non-Jewish groups, including evangelical Christian ones, also use the *kibbutz* as a means to introduce their young people to the land. These young people often volunteer their labor in exchange for room and board. During their off-hours, they are able to tour the country. Many have enjoyed the *kibbutz* experience so much they have made *aliya* and moved to Israel permanently as a result of these programs.

Kibbutzim are organized according to their social and religious characters. There are four federations:

(1) Union of Collective Settlement
   (*Ihud ha-Kevuzot ve-ha-Kibbutzim*)

(2) The National Kibbutz Movement
   (*Ha-Kibbutz ha-Arzi-ha-Za'ir*)

(3) United Kibbutz Movement
   (*Ha-Kibbutz ha-Me'uhad*)

(4) The Religious Kibbutz
   (*Ha-Kibbuz ha-Dati*)

These groups pool their resources and work together to accomplish mutually agreed-on goals.

Another type of community village found in Israel is called the *moshav*, begun as a compromise between a family-owned farm or business and a *kibbutz*. The first two *moshavim* were founded in

1921 by families who liked the *kibbutz* concept but wanted to keep the family together. The *moshav* became a viable alternative for some of the newer immigrants who felt threatened by the way *kibbutz* communities function. On *moshavim*, families pool their resources and cooperate in producing goods or crops, then distribute the profits among themselves.

Nearly ninety years have passed since the founding of the first *kibbutz*. If you lived on a *kibbutz*, you would probably say, "It is not an ideal society, but a society of ideals,"[4] a place that offers security while demanding loyalty and diligence. Most would agree that it has proved to be a stable and reliable institution that has given *kibbutzniks* a family atmosphere and the satisfaction of knowing they have worked for the good of their country and their people.

LOST HOPE RECLAIMED

HA-TIKVAH (THE HOPE)

Kol od baleivay p'nima
(As long as deep within the heart)
Nefesh Y'hudi homiya
(The Jewish soul is warm)
Ul'fa-atey mizrach kadima
(And toward the edges of the east)
Ayin L'Tziyon tzofiya
(An eye to Zion looks)
Od lo avada tikvateynu
(Our hope is not yet lost)
Hatikva sh'not alpayim
(The hope is not yet lost)
Lih'yot am chofshi b'artzenu
(To be a free people in our own land)
Eretz Tziyon v'yirushalayim
(In the land of Zion and Jerusalem)
Lih'yot am chofshi b'artzenu
(To be a free people in our own land)
Eretz Tzion v'yirushalayim.
(In the land of Zion and Jerusalem.)

Then he said unto me, Son of man, these bones are the
whole house of Israel; behold, they say, Our bones are
dried, and our hope is lost; we are cut off on our part
(Ezek. 37:11).

THE NAME EZEKIEL MEANS "GOD will strengthen." As he stood
staring into a valley strewn with scattered, dry, sun-scorched
bones, Ezekiel certainly needed a large infusion of God's
strength. The heart-wrenching lament the prophet-priest heard
made him realize that his people had lost all hope.

As Ezekiel prophesied to his captive people, an unnamed
compatriot and psalmist poetically described the emotions of the
Jewish exiles in Babylon:

By the rivers of Babylon, there we sat down, yea, we
wept, when we remembered Zion. We hung our harps
upon the willows in the midst thereof.... How shall we
sing the LORD's song in a foreign land? (Ps. 137:1–2, 4)

In his commentary on this psalm, the late Bible expositor
J. Vernon McGee captured the plight of the Jewish people. Dr.
McGee wrote,

These people have had an experience that no other peo-
ple have had. From the land of Goshen to the ghettos of
Europe they have known what it is to be away from
their homeland, to be in a strange land. They know
what it is to go all the way from the brickyards of Egypt
to Babylonian canals. They know what it is to spend
time in slave labor camps. By the rivers of Babylon was
a place where they were persecuted, where they per-
formed slave labor, a place they suffered.[1]

McGee continued: "With a sob in their soul they said, 'We've
lost our song.'" This condition, as debilitating and frightening as
lost breath, hovered like a cloud over the Jewish people well
beyond the rivers of Babylon. Jewish history abounds with
accounts of persecution, torture, and expulsion from lands the

Jewish people had tried in vain to call home. For more than two thousand years, they wandered the earth—the unfortunate, often unwelcome guests in various Gentile lands. Could their lost hope ever be regained?

As the nineteenth century drew to a close, things were taking place that indicated the dead bones in Ezekiel's ancient vision were beginning to shake, just as he had been told they would (37:2–7). Those noisy, moving, yet lifeless bones were the various gifted Jewish people—still separated by space, age, and time—who were following an almost mysterious call to unite the people without a land to the land without a people.

Men like Theodor Herzl, Eliezer Ben-Yehuda, David Ben-Gurion, and Chaim Weizman were among the many who championed the remedy for lost Jewish hope—Zionism, the movement for a national Jewish homeland in *Eretz Yisrael*, the land God had promised as an everlasting possession to the descendants of Abraham, Isaac, and Jacob. With an almost spiritual fervor, they provided the energy needed to bring the bones together.

One such champion wrote a poem that Jewish people around the world would memorize and even sing. Originally titled *Tkvatenu* (Our Hope), it later was renamed *Ha-tikvah* (The Hope). It was written around 1878 by Romanian Naphtali Hetrz Imber, published in 1886, and eventually set to music. Somehow, the singing of *Ha-tikvah* infused an energy and enthusiasm into the dry, parched, and scattered bones of Ezekiel's 2,500-year-old vision, gathering them into a great and standing army. *Ha-tikvah* became a rallying song and, eventually, the national anthem of the resurrected, modern State of Israel.

Born in 1856, Naphtali Hetrz Imber was considered a child prodigy, excelling in Hebraic and Talmudic studies. He began writing poetry at age ten. His great abilities in Jewish studies provided opportunities for him to travel to such places as Paris, Berlin, London, Bombay, Palestine, and even New York. His visits to these faraway cities of the world inspired him to write many of his essays, prose, and poems.

From 1882 to 1886, Imber served as secretary and adviser on Jewish affairs in Palestine under Christian-Zionist Laurence Oliphant.[2] He immediately fell in love with the place, rock-strewn and barren though it was at that time. The experience so changed him that he devoted the rest of his life to enabling his people to return to *Eretz Yisrael.*

At the same time, this same yearning seized thousands of Jews around the world. Many left countries they were living in to make the difficult and dangerous journey home. As Imber traveled the countryside visiting the various Jewish colonies and communities, he often stopped to read his poem to these pioneers and settlers. The words of *Ha-tikvah* moved them immensely, encouraging them to continue their struggle to secure their homeland. Imber added several stanzas to his work, inspired by the reception it had when he read it. Many of these farming communities already had adopted a poem or song for the very purpose of uniting and encouraging them in their cause. One such community, Rehovot, established in 1890, chose *Ha-tikvah* as its anthem.

The origins of the haunting music attached to the poem are somewhat of a mystery. Some say it can be traced to "The Bohemian Symphony" by Czech composer Smetana—strains of the melody can be heard throughout the work. Others say it is based on the Sephardic melody for Psalm 117 in the Hallel service.[3] Or perhaps the composer was Samuel Cohen, a Moldavian immigrant and resident of Rehovot who used a Romanian tune. No one seems to know for sure.

In 1897, at the first Zionist Congress in Basle, Switzerland, delegates determined that a national anthem would be needed for the future Zionist state. Theodor Herzl and Max Nordau decided to hold a competition to find a suitable one. The entries reportedly were so bad that Herzl ordered the contest canceled and the entries destroyed.

The next year, in 1898, Herzl visited the Jewish community of Rehovot and heard the singing of *Ha-tikvah.* He was so impressed with the song that he had it performed at the 1901 Zionist Congress in Romania. Informally adopted as the official song of the Congress in 1905, it caught on quickly and soon became a song of the people throughout the land of Palestine. In 1933 the Zionist Congress met and confirmed *Ha-tikvah* as the official anthem of the Zionist movement.

Soon the song's melodious strains could be heard throughout the land, stirring so much emotion and passion among the Palestinian Jews that the British who controlled the land banned it. As a result of that action, the forbidden song became a rallying call for an underground movement throughout the country. When Israel declared its statehood in 1948, it was sung as the national anthem. Except for a bill tabled by the Knesset in 1967 that would have made the song "Jerusalem of Gold" the anthem, *Ha-tikvah* has never been challenged and remains the national anthem of Israel today. It is an interesting reflection on Israel's history and population in that it was written, not by a Hebrew-speaking *Sabra* (native born Israeli), but by a Romanian-speaking member of the Diaspora (scattered Jews) who, himself, possessed that great hope for a homeland.

There are those who believe that *Ha-tikvah* should not be the anthem because, like America's "Star Spangled Banner," it is difficult to play and sing. Yet world-renowned musician Zubin Mehta, former conductor of the Israel Symphony, has called it the most beautiful anthem on earth.

An almost indescribable feeling comes over most Jewish people today when *Ha-tikvah* is sung. Somehow the lyrics possess the power to restore the hope so many of them have lost through thousands of years of tragic history.

The poem says, "The hope of two thousand years, to be free, A free people in our land, Our hope is not lost." *Ha-tikva* is an anthem able to unite the Jewish political and/or religious right with the Jewish political and/or religious left. For more than one hundred years, *Ha-tikvah* has been reclaiming hope for the Jewish people.

Imber, who died in 1908, wrote *Ha-tikvah* when there was no Israel and there were no Israelis. The overwhelming majority of the Jewish people had been dispossessed of their God-given land for almost two thousand years. The only Hebrew spoken was in synagogues on the Sabbath or some other feast day. Today every Jewish person in the world is entitled to citizenship in this land given to their father Abraham—a land where Hebrew is spoken in homes, on streets, and in the seat of government as well as in synagogues.

What power could accomplish that monumental feat? The answer is found in the heart of chapter 37 of Ezekiel, verse 12:

> *I will open your graves, and cause you to come up out of your graves, and bring you into the land of Israel.*

As wonderful as it may be that Jewish people today can stand proudly before the flag of Israel and sing *Ha-tikvah*, a future day will bring something far more glorious. In Ezekiel 37:14 God promises,

> *And [I] shall put my Spirit in you, and ye shall live, and I shall place you in your own land; then shall ye know that I, the LORD, have spoken it, and performed it, saith the LORD.*

THE MAN WHO BROUGHT
HEBREW BACK TO THE LAND

FOR ITS FIRST ISSUE OF THE YEAR 2000, *The Jerusalem Report*, a prominent international Jewish magazine, published the results of a poll in which it asked its readers to choose the one hundred greatest Jews of the past millennium. Four of the top ten were David Ben-Gurion, Theodor Herzl, Yitzhak Rabin, and Golda Meir. No doubt these well-known individuals placed high because of the indisputably monumental contributions they made to the establishment and growth of the modern State of Israel.

At the same time, however, it was rather disappointing that the man who brought Hebrew back to the land only came in thirty-eighth. His name was Eliezer Ben-Yehuda, a man with every bit as much Zionistic fervor as those in the top four. And his accomplishment may well have eclipsed all others save that of Herzl himself, the father of Zionism.

Ben-Yehuda's zeal as a Zionist came many years before Herzl's. I remember a story I once heard when I was a young boy attending Hebrew school. It beautifully sums up the magnitude of Ben-Yehuda's achievement. Around 1897, when the first Zionist Congress met, a legion of skeptics found it incredulous that the Jewish people could ever be reestablished in their land as a viable country in the world. Many poked fun at Herzl and his supporters. One such critic asserted that there was as much chance of creating a modern Jewish state as there was that the people in that state would all speak Hebrew—the ancient tongue of Israel.

His cynicism was understandable. At that time, Hebrew was virtually a dead language. Generally, only biblical scholars used it, and even they rarely conversed in it because thousands of words used every day in other languages simply did not exist in Hebrew. There was, for example, no way to say bicycle or doll or ice cream or bulldozer.

But Ben-Yehuda was not to be deterred. His goal was *Yisrael b'artzo uvilshono*—Israel in its own land, speaking its own language.

Eliezer Yitzhak Perelman, as he was named at his birth in 1858, was born in Luzhky, Lithuania. Reared in a Hasidic household, he was able to attend *yeshivah* (Jewish day school) despite the fact his father had died when he was only five years old. Living at a time when *haskala*—enlightenment— was sweeping Europe, Eliezer became very interested in secular literature, a heresy for Hasidic Jews. As a result, he was expelled from his uncle's home, where he had been living, and had to find lodging elsewhere. He moved to Vilna and lived in the home of a Hasidic scholar who also had been influenced by the enlightenment.

While there, he learned to read and write several languages and became more and more influenced by the European awakening. In an unfinished autobiography, Ben-Yehuda told of that time and its profound effect on him. The following excerpt came from an article written by Ben-Yehuda's grandson and cited on the Internet by Lev Software of Ft. Lauderdale, Florida. In it, Ben-Yehuda detailed an experience that changed the direction of his life forever.

In those days it was as if the heavens had suddenly opened, and a clear, incandescent light flashed before my eyes and a mighty inner voice sounded in my ears 'the resurrection of Israel on its ancestral soil.' Because of that voice, which has not ceased from that moment on to ring in my ears day and night, all my thoughts and plans which I had for my future life were shaken up. As night visions pale in the face of the light of day, so were my dreams of dedicating my life to the cause of freedom in the Russian nation replaced with a single ideal, manifest in the Hebrew words 'Yisrael b'artzo'— Israel in its own land! I was challenged by many, and one argument said that the Jews are not now and could not be in the future a nation—because they did not possess a common tongue . . . the more I thought of the national revival the more I realized what a tongue can do to unite a people. I realized that just as the Jews could not become a living nation except by returning to their ancient homeland—so also they could not become a living nation except by returning to the language of their ancestors, speaking it not only in prayer and study but also in all matters of life, young and old alike, at all hours of the day and night—just like every other nation, each with its tongue. That was the decisive moment in my life, when I saw that the two things without which the Jews could not become a nation are the land and the language![1]

In 1878 Ben-Yehuda made the decision to move from Paris, where he was living, and settle in *Eretz Yisrael*—the land of Israel. At the time, the land was a virtual Babel of languages. Under Turkish rule, the various tongues included Arabic, Russian, Yiddish, English, and some Hebrew. Ben-Yehuda desired to start a community of Hebrew speakers who actually lived in the land. In religious circles, however, Hebrew was considered too sacred to speak on a daily basis so there was objection to the idea of vulgarizing its sanctity.

Ben-Yehudah's seemingly far-fetched plans seemed even more unlikely when he contracted tuberculosis in the winter of 1878. While in the hospital in Paris, he met A. M. Lunz, a man who spoke impeccable Sephardi Hebrew. Sephardi Hebrew was used in the transliteration of biblical names in ancient and modern translations of the Bible.

By 1881, not fully recovered from the effects of his illness but with his vision for a "people wedded to a land, speaking its own language," he began his journey to Jerusalem.[2] Having broken off a relationship with his childhood sweetheart because of his illness, Eliezer was shocked to see her waiting for him in Vienna. She was prepared to make the rest of the journey to the Holy Land with him as his wife. When he reminded her of the difficulties that lay ahead, Deborah responded as Ruth had responded to her mother-in-law, Naomi, hundreds of years before: "Wherever you go, I will go; and where you lodge I will lodge."[3] They were married in Cairo.

When they landed in Jaffa in October 1881, Eliezar informed his wife that they would no longer speak Russian. From that moment forward, Hebrew would be their only language. His new bride replied in Russian, "I do not speak Hebrew." His answer: "Then you will be silent in Hebrew."[4] Theirs became the first Hebrew-speaking home established in Jerusalem and their son, born in 1882, the first modern-Hebrew-speaking child.

Ben-Yehuda established a society whose goal was to revive the language in the land. He wrote for a political magazine and taught in a Jerusalem school where he was permitted to instruct in Hebrew—the first school in the land with such instruction. He published a geography book called *Eretz Yisrael* and translated many texts for use in the classroom on subjects such as math and literature. He wrote for *Hakhavatzelet*, a Hebrew literary periodical, and launched *Hatzvi*, a weekly newspaper published in Hebrew that reported the news of the land. Soon the need grew to create words that did not already exist in Hebrew. So Ben-Yehuda published lists of words he fabricated. In fact, when he began to publish a dictionary, the word *dictionary* did not exist.

In 1891 his faithful wife, Deborah, died of tuberculosis, leaving him with two small children. According to the account written by Eliezer's grandson, Deborah wrote a letter to her younger sister shortly before her death: "If you want to be a queen," she said, "then hurry to Jerusalem and marry my prince, my darling Eliezer."[5] And her sister did. She changed her name to *Hemda* ("darling" in Hebrew) and made the journey to Jerusalem. Six months later they were married. She helped him immensely in his work and supported him in all he did.

Ben-Yehuda founded and presided over Va'ad HaLashon, the forerunner of the Hebrew Language Academy, while working tirelessly on his dictionary.[6] In 1910 he published the first six volumes. He died in 1922 without completing his work. His wife and son Ehud (whose son, in turn, wrote the material used by Lev Software) continued publishing his manuscript—a task that was not finished until 1959, long after their deaths. In all, seventeen volumes were completed, listing all the words used in Hebrew literature from the time of Abraham to modern times.

To understand this immense accomplishment, one has only to think of biblical prophecy. One day the Messiah of Israel will return to His people, the Jewish people. When He touches down on the Mount of Olives, walks down and up the slopes of the Valley of Kidron and through the gates of the old city walls, He will seat Himself on the throne of His father David. When that happens, the language He will hear, and possibly even speak, will once again be Hebrew—the language of His kinsmen according to the flesh.

The story of Israel is a story of resurrection. There is but one nation in the world whose people were forced to leave their homeland, to survive more than nineteen hundred years in other countries, and to finally come home. As incredible as that miracle is—and it is a miracle—it is no less a miracle that the national language today is, once again, Hebrew.

Eliezer Ben-Yehuda may have been thirty-eighth on one list, but he is number one on mine.

THE FIRST LINE OF DEFENSE

ONCE A YEAR AN ORTHODOX COMMUNITY in Israel assembles to honor the boys from fatherless families who are ready for bar mitzvah. The fathers of these boys all lost their lives in service to their country. On one such occasion twenty-three years ago, a young boy nicknamed Shai was chosen to deliver the special address to this assembly. Shai (meaning "gift") is the name his mother lovingly called him because she felt he was an extra special gift to her. Shai never knew his father because he had died in Syria just a few weeks before Shai's birth.

In his speech, Shai said he would have liked to have been like other children because then, he said, "I would have had a father whom I knew and who lived with us like other fathers." Shai then spoke not to the guests, but directly to his father when he said, "I promise you, Father, that in my life I will never fail you. I will do my duty with all my strength and my devotion to the nation of Israel."[1] There was not a dry eye in the synagogue.

Such courage and devotion help explain Israel's survival and testify to the tenacity of her people and the faithfulness of her God. Hostile nations so dwarf the country that it is even difficult to locate the Jewish nation on a world map. Former Prime

Minister Benjamin Netanyahu provides a startling statistic in his book *A Place Among the Nations* (Bantam). Beneath a chart of four facsimiles of recognizable land masses, he lists the number of square miles each area encompasses:

Israel	10,840
California	160,000
France	213,613
Iraq	280,000[2]

Population differential is also striking. Currently, the total population of Israel just breaches six million people, of which about five million are Jewish. The neighboring Middle Eastern communities number about 150 million people, most of them Muslims. If the Middle East were a place of serenity and peace, size and population differences would be insignificant. But many years of turbulent Israeli history prove that Israel's enemies would like nothing more than to drive the Jewish homeland into the Mediterranean Sea.

Throughout its fifty-two years of existence, Israel has relied more on its knowledge of enemy activities than on its artillery, jets, and missiles. Espionage—the gathering of accurate and reliable knowledge—is regarded as a first line of defense.

Espionage is not new to Israel's history. Thousands of years ago, God directed Moses to send out twelve undercover agents to foreign soil for a fact-finding mission: "Send thou men, that they may search the land of Canaan, which I give unto the children of Israel" (Num. 13:2). They were to "see the land, what it is; and the people who dwell therein, whether they are strong or weak, few or many" (Num. 13:18). The only difference from then until now is that now, twelve men are simply not enough.

Included in this first line of defense is an organization called The Institute for Intelligence and Special Tasks, comprised of an estimated fifteen hundred people. Better known as Mossad, it was birthed in its present form by the late Prime Minister David Ben-Gurion at the time Israel became a nation. Its responsibilities include human intelligence, covert action, and counterterrorism. To be successful, the work must be accomplished unnoticed. Yet there have been times when Mossad's success has been so amazing that secrecy was impossible.

One of the Mossad's most brilliant coups involved the capture of Adolf Eichmann, whose name even today sends shivers down the spines of most Jewish people. As chief of the Jewish Office of the Gestapo and prime architect of Hitler's "Final Solution," Eichmann was responsible for engineering the deaths of millions of Jewish people. While many Nazi criminals were brought to trial after World War II, Eichmann managed to hide his identity and elude capture. In 1959, fourteen years after the war had ended, the elusive Eichmann was finally found. Although a painstakingly difficult and intricate case, Mossad was able to accumulate the information necessary to pinpoint his exact location, a house on Garibaldi Street in Buenos Aires, Argentina.

To capture and extricate him from the country required precision down to the minutest detail. It was necessary that Eichmann appear to be leaving Argentina voluntarily. Thus the plan required a partially drugged Eichmann to walk through the airport and board an El Al plane destined for Israel.

Commenting on his capture and kidnapping, Eichmann himself stated, "My capture was carried out in a sporting fashion and was outstanding for its organization and exemplary planning."[3]

In May of 1960, David Ben-Gurion made an emotional announcement to the Knesset: "I have to announce that . . . one of the greatest of Nazi criminals was found by Israeli secret service: Adolf Eichmann, who was responsible, together with the Nazi leaders, for what they called the 'Final Solution to the Jewish Problem.'"[4] His capture, trial, conviction, and execution were an integral step toward healing a people scarred by the Holocaust.

Espionage is dangerous, daunting, and difficult because it requires pilfering information while in enemy territory.

Nevertheless, Israel has managed many successful and even amazing thefts of enemy hardware in enemy country. The Russians, for example, had been supplying Israel's enemies with top-secret Mig planes, which were superior to anything in the Israeli Air Force. Israel needed to capture one for defense purposes. In an operation carried out in 1966, the unbelievable became believable when a female Mossad agent convinced an Iraqi pilot to fly a top-secret, Russian Mig directly to Israel. The complex operation required smuggling the pilot's family out of Iraq to safety in Israel, planning the timing and execution of the theft, and secluding the pilot after completion of the mission. That theft provided military intelligence with valuable information that later helped Israel win the Six-Day War. Israel also shared the knowledge gained from the seizure with her best friend—the United States.

Of all the stories told about Israel's Mossad, the account of the work of Eliahu (Elie) Cohn is among the most well-known. To this day, the book *Our Man in Damascus*, the story of Elie Cohn, is a must-read for any tourist to Israel.

Born into an Orthodox Jewish home in Alexandria, Egypt, on December 16, 1924, Elie seemed destined for the rabbinate. He became a star pupil in the Hebrew school run by the chief rabbi. His keen mind also helped him in secular school, earning him a scholarship to the French high school in Alexandria where he excelled in mathematics and engineering. His gift of memorization enabled him to become fluent in several languages.

During World War II, Egypt's loyalties were divided between the Allies and the Nazis. Due to increasing anti-Semitism, many Jews tried to immigrate to Palestine. Elie helped the Haganah, the military of the pre-state of Israel, to smuggle many Egyptian Jews into their national homeland. He always considered himself a loyal Egyptian; and in 1947, just one year before Israel was forced to fight for her independence, Elie enlisted in the Egyptian army. But the military declared him ineligible due to "mixed loyalties," undoubtedly alleged because he was Jewish.

The anti-Semitic atmosphere in Egypt did not prevent the brilliant Elie from earning an engineering degree in 1950. By then he was convinced that being Jewish and Egyptian were not compatible. So when Israeli intelligence approached him to work for them, he accepted. His command of languages made him extremely effective. Elie remained in Egypt through the Sinai campaign of 1956. When he was discovered working for the Jewish state, he had to flee for his life into Israel.

There he applied for a job with Mossad but was rejected, not realizing that Mossad never hires unless it initiates the contact. Elie was disappointed. His knowledge of the business world, however, enabled him to get a job as an accountant. For the next three years, Mossad watched as Elie settled into Israeli life and into his marriage in 1959. His work in Egypt was noticed and appreciated, but Mossad needed to watch him as he adjusted to life in Israel.

Evidently Mossad was satisfied, for in 1960 Elie Cohn was hired, this time on Mossad's initiative. After six months of extensive training, Elie Cohn was sent to Syria. In 1961, Egypt and Syria were Israel's foremost enemies. Elie was a perfect fit for this assignment because he spoke perfect Arabic and had excellent knowledge of the customs of the Arab people. His assignment was to infiltrate the Syrian military. He was to pose as an exporter, using the name Kamil Amin Taabes. As Kamil Amin Taabes, Elie established himself in Argentina as a wealthy businessman. His cover was meticulously fabricated by the Mossad. With the success of the Eichmann kidnapping, many countries were particularly suspicious of anyone who was allowed near classified information. The Syrians carefully scrutinized Kamil's identity while he was living in Argentina, and he passed with flying colors.

Elie managed to smuggle into Syria a radio transmitter that relayed information to Tel Aviv regularly. Kamil had become a confidant to a number of high-ranking Syrian officials and ingratiated himself to his many friends with parties and entertainment, keeping a closed mouth about their social activities.

Over a two-year span, he was often taken to high security areas, including the Golan Heights, a mountainous range on the eastern coast of the Sea of Galilee. Militarily, this was a superior piece of real estate for Syria because it was ideally situated for bombarding Israel. The Syrians had placed thousands of land mines, bunkers, and key military installations there and were constantly terrorizing the Israeli kibbutzim down below.

Kamil was given total freedom to walk the Golan and gaze down at Israel. To demonstrate his support for Syria, Kamil encouraged its leadership to plant trees over the bunkers to provide shade and camouflage for them. His suggestions were implemented.

Thanks to his acute memory, Elie was able to radio exact information for locating enemy targets. He remained on the Syrian scene on and off for about four years. Although Mossad had felt for some time that Elie should come home, Elie felt he should stay a little longer. In January of 1965, a little longer proved too long.

A crack military team came crashing through his door while he was broadcasting information to Israel. Unknown to him, all radio messages had been temporarily halted, making it possible for Syria to trace his transmission.

Elie Cohn was tortured, then executed by hanging. He had so greatly embarrassed the Syrians that they did not permit the normal negotiations for captured spies. Even Israel's offer of one million dollars for his body was denied.

But Elie's contribution to his country lived on. The information he provided was invaluable for helping Israel win the Golan Heights in 1967. Israeli jet pilots received instructions to bomb the trees. They were the eucalyptus trees planted at Elie's suggestion. They clearly identified every Syrian bunker, thus providing Israel with a high percentage of direct hits on enemy targets. Elie Cohn was a national hero. But he was also one of many soldiers whose wives became widows and whose children became fatherless.

That is why the words spoken at the bar mitzvah in the Orthodox community were particularly moving. The young man nicknamed Shai, who spoke so eloquently to the father he never knew, pledging to him his devotion to Israel, was Shaul Cohn, the son of Elie Cohn, born just weeks before his father's death.

It was a difficult speech to give because he knew the pain of even mentioning his father in the presence of his mother. In the audience that day was Menachem Begin, the prime minister of Israel, who was moved to tears. Mossad continues even now to provide Israel's first line of defense.

But there will come a day when Israel will have everlasting peace with God's sanctuary in its midst forever (Ezek. 37:26). One day, when Messiah comes, Israel will no longer need a Mossad. That will be a blessed day!

ARE THERE HORNS UNDER THAT HAT? MYTHS ABOUT THE JEWISH PEOPLE

MANY YEARS AGO THERE WAS A series on American television called *Little House on the Prairie*. One of the show's characters, a youngster named Albert, became friendly with an elderly Jewish man. The children at school made fun of Albert because they ignorantly believed many falsehoods about the Jewish people.

One of the things they told Albert was to beware of what was concealed under the man's hat. Being an observant Jew, the man consistently wore a head covering, a sign of his reverence for God. The children said he was hiding his horns. (Many people believed that the Jewish people were demonic.) Albert did not want to believe his friends, but he had never met a Jewish person before, so he wanted to be sure. He tried different ways to get the man to remove his hat, but to no avail. Finally, he told the old man what his schoolmates had said. The old man smiled, took off his hat, and, to Albert's relief and embarrassment, there were no horns. This fictional story, set in the late 1800s, brought out a myth about Jewish people that goes back to the Middle Ages.

Michelangelo is one of the most famous artists in history. His frescoes on the ceiling of the Sistine Chapel in the Vatican are world renowned. His marble sculpture of the great Jewish king, David, is magnificent. In 1515 Michelangelo finished a sculpture of the great Jewish prophet, Moses, complete with horns protruding from his head. Although the horns sculpted onto Moses' head were the result of an unfortunate mistranslation of a word in the Latin Vulgate, the statue has perpetuated the horns myth since the Middle Ages.

Many who view Michelangelo's Moses and the fictional characters living on the prairie have been exposed to a *myth*, which is defined by *Merriam Webster's Collegiate Dictionary* as "an unfounded or false notion." The Jewish people have long been the target of myths. It is these false notions that have been used to deny one of the most documented events in all of human history, the Nazi Holocaust. At the root of each of these myths is the venom of anti-Semitism. It can be camouflaged and cloaked to look like superstition or fairy tale, but, as Adolf Hitler said, "Make the lie big make it simple, keep saying it, and eventually they will believe it." When combined with existing prejudice, that process does not take long.

Misconstrued theology is also at the root of various myths about the Jewish people. Although Jesus was a Jew, lived in Israel, and chose Jewish disciples, and although the first Christians were Jewish, there arose the belief over time that God had rejected His people. The Temple, destroyed in A.D. 70, was used as "proof" of this rejection. It later would be argued that the Jewish people killed Christ; thus, the "new Israel," meaning, the church, would take the place of the Temple. This false theology was a starting point for prejudice against the Jewish people.

The list of religious leaders who used Bible verses to justify anti-Semitic statements runs long. John Chrysostom, who lived in the late 300s, said that Jewish people were a disease capable of contaminating the population. Martin Luther, the great reformer who at one time called on Christians to treat the Jews kindly, later wrote a book in which he called the Jews, among other things, thieves and vermin. He also called for the burning of Jewish books and synagogues. Irenaeus, Bishop of Lyon, declared that the Jews were "disinherited from the grace of God" and "would never have hesitated to burn their own Jewish scriptures."[1]

During the Middle Ages, Jewish people were seen as greedy, dirty, and diseased liars. They were viewed as conspirators with Satan, as the enemies of the church. As aimless wanderers, their very existence was said to mean the downfall of their host nation. Myths of an intrinsically evil character, including accusing them of a conspiracy to defeat Gentiles, have stuck like glue to the Jewish people.

No wonder they were accused of poisoning wells, spreading diseases such as the black plague, and stealing away children as sacrifices for their worship.

Perpetuating these myths was rather simple, since Judaism taught a separatist lifestyle. As time passed, Gentiles grew more and more ignorant of Jewish traditions and faith. Ignorance of this biblical people, as well as of the Bible itself, proved to be a breeding ground for fear. Legal restrictions were passed by various nations requiring distinctive dress or symbols on the clothing of Jews to alert people about them. Segregation became a way of life for many Jewish people.

It must be remembered that many countries allowed the Jews to thrive. Yet, while things might go well for a time, all it took was some difficulty, some inexplicable problem, to provide a reason to persecute the Jewish people. Thus, the Crusades, Inquisition, and pogroms were burned into Jewish history.

A document written at the turn of the 20th century entitled *The Protocols of the Learned Elders of Zion* played on the myth of a Jewish conspiracy. Its thesis was simple and direct: The Jews are plotting to take over the world. Proven to be a forgery of a work by Maurice Jolly written in 1864 to demonstrate Napoleon's delusions of world domination, the *Protocols* have been labeled a "pretext and rationale for anti-Semitism" even by the *Encyclopaedia Britannica*. But the *Protocols* influenced such men as

Henry Ford, who published excerpts in his *Dearborn Independent* newspaper, as well as in a book entitled *The International Jew*. The *Protocols* are still sold today, usually through ads in blatantly anti-Semitic magazines. It is common fodder for those who believe the Holocaust to be a lie. It was also required reading in Germany during the days of the Third Reich.

Employing the character myth makes it easy for deniers to explain away the volumes of proof for the Holocaust. When asked to explain the reasoning behind making the Jews wear yellow stars on their clothes to identify them in European communities, Robert Faurission, former professor of literature at the University of Lyons #2 and a Holocaust denier, claims that it was a measure designed to protect the German soldiers. The Jews, he said, engaged in terrorism, black market arms trafficking, other dangerous activities. According to Faurission, Jewish men, women, and children were a "formidable enemy."[2] Austin App, professor of English at the University of Scranton at La Salle, concluded that the majority of the Jews who supposedly died at German hands were, in fact, "subversives, partisans, spies, saboteurs, and criminals."[3] Others with lesser credentials have asserted that the Jews simply lie about the Holocaust or that those few who did die deserved their fate because they were enemies of the Germans.[4]

It seems incredible that a people with such a formidable army, who talked about ruling for a thousand years, had to go on the offensive against a people scattered throughout many different countries with no army, no political organization, and no homeland. Yet the reasons given by those who deny the Holocaust emphasize the enormous power that the Germans seemed to need for protection from what they considered an innately evil and powerful people.

The conspiracy myth is often used to try to negate the mounds of hard evidence for the occurrence of the Holocaust. The assertion is that the Jews, Bolsheviks, and Communists all worked together in the "hoax" to swindle money from West Germany.

The Jews are not the "victims but the victimizers,"[5] spreading the hoax to win international sympathy and thus accomplish their secret goals. The Americans and British joined in on the conspiracy because they, so it is asserted, killed thousands of civilians with their indiscriminate bombings.

To have been able to spread all these lies, the deniers claim that the Jews control the media. Paul Rassinier asserts, "The Jews have been able to dupe the world by relying on their mythic powers and conspiratorial abilities. As they have so often done in the past, world Jewry has once again employed its inordinate powers to harness the world's financial resources, media, and political interests for their own purposes."[6]

The following are examples of some of the incredible accusations leveled against traditional historians.

MYTH: SIX MILLION DID NOT DIE; THAT IS A JEWISH EXAGGERATION

I do not know of anyone—expert, scholar, or lay person—who believes that there were exactly six million Jewish deaths. In fact, it is Jewish scholars who continue to investigate information relating to the Holocaust. The actual number of deaths is difficult to extrapolate because many of the numbers have been gathered from the Germans themselves. I have seen numbers as low as 5.2 million and as high as 5.95 million. The number six million has been used as a general estimation. Adolf Eichmann, chief of the deportation system for the Nazis, estimated "that a total of two million, five hundred thousand died in Auschwitz alone."[7] "Estimates on the Einsatzgruppen murders run as high as 3.5 million."[8] These killer units were designed to "kill on the road."

These statistics alone add up to more than five million. It is important to realize that questioning the exact number misses the point. What would be the reason to single out a group of people—men, women, and children, all living in different countries—and target them for extermination?

MYTH: THERE WERE NO GAS CHAMBERS, AND ZYKLON-B GAS COULD NOT HAVE BEEN USED

Actually, there were two kinds of extermination chambers. The first was a mobile unit, or truck, used by the Einsatzgruppen. People were told they had to wash and have their clothes disinfected. Then the exhaust pipe was vented into the middle of the floor. This information came from interrogation of SS members themselves.

The gas chambers at Auschwitz not only existed but functioned on a regular basis. Written diaries from Jewish people, records from the Nazis (including work orders, supply requisitions, time sheets, engineering instructions, invoices, and completion reports), and testimonies from *sonderkommandos* (attendants) all corroborate their existence.

Testimonies of Nazis, prisoners, and sonderkommandos also indicate that anyone involved with moving out the dead did so wearing gas masks. In addition, those who say Zyklon-B gas was not used rationalize that it is too toxic. Yet they themselves claim the same gas was used for disinfection. Disinfection is carried out with a bactericide, not an insecticide.[9]

The fictional TV character Albert and millions of others have lived among people who believed lies perpetrated by individuals who were at best ignorant and at worst filled with hate. Albert had the courage to ask the old Jewish man to remove his hat. He didn't allow ignorance, fear, or prejudice to get the better of him for long. Michelangelo's mistakenly horned statue of Moses, on the other hand, continues to promote the ignorance and prejudice that fuels the passions of anti-Semites.

The myths surrounding the denial of the Holocaust are rooted in the myths that people have believed for centuries to be true of the Jewish people. Anti-Semitism and Holocaust denial are synonymous entities. The only way to confront these entities is with truth—the truth of the Word of God and the truth of history.

When I visited Israel, I had the privilege of eating at the home of our correspondent, Zvi. I told him that I taught a course on the

Holocaust. His reply: "Talk to me. I know about this." Then I asked him about those who deny that it ever took place. He said, "Bring them to me." Of all the evidences to rebuff the myths, this flesh-and-blood survivor, and others like him, is the best of all proof.

THOSE WHO DIED . . .

COUNTRY	PRE-WAR JEWISH POPULATION	NUMBER OF JEWISH PEOPLE KILLED
Baltic	250,000	230,000
Belgium	90,000	40,000
Bulgaria	65,000	15,000
Denmark	8,000	N/A
Finland	2,000	N/A
France	300,000	90,000
Germany/Austria	785,000	210,000
Greece	75,000	60,000
Hungary	650,000	450,000
Italy	40,000	8,000
Luxembourg	5,000	1,000
Netherlands	150,000	120,000
Norway	2,000	800
Poland	3,334,000	2,940,000
USSR		
Russia	975,0001	107,000
Ukraine	1,500,000	900,000
White Russia	375,000	245,000
Romania	850,000	425,000
Slovakia	90,000	70,000
Yugoslavia	75,000	55,000
TOTAL	**9,621,000**	**5,966,800**

(Figures taken from *Encountering the Holocaust* by Bryron L. Sherwin and Susan G. Ament.)

Is the New Testament
Anti-Semitic?

IF I HAD BEEN ASKED, "IS THE NEW Testament anti-Semitic?" during my university years, I would not have hesitated a moment before answering, "Yes!"

My formative years were spent surrounded by people whose perception of "that book" was of its inherent evil and dangerous intent. As far as I was concerned, my people experienced years of bitter suffering as a direct result of the contents of that Gentile Bible. Interestingly, I had never read it. In fact, I could not imagine even touching its pages. Yet I was sure that humiliating and hateful terms, such as "Christ killers" and "children of the Devil," were quoted from it. Today many people have this perception of the New Testament, and by no means are all of them Jewish.

What many believe the New Testament teaches is summarized as follows:

> God chose the Jewish people, but they were disobedient;
> and when God sent them prophets, Israel rejected and
> killed them. These prophets promised a Redeemer
> would come who would be God in the flesh. When

> *Jesus came, they rejected and killed him. So their Temple was destroyed and God rejected them. God then chose another people to take the Jews' place. These people gladly received Jesus and, as a result, will spend eternity in the presence of God.*

Undoubtedly, this perception has motivated various Gentile nations and individuals to oppress Jewish people down through the millennia.

Rabbi Eliezar Berkovits said, "Christianity's New Testament has been the most dangerous anti-Semitic tract in history."[1] Another rabbi has said, "I believe the New Testament is a factor in anti-Semitism today as in the past."[2] Similar thoughts also are held by a group of "theologians" who desire to delete what they believe are anti-Jewish sections of the New Testament. According to an article by Paul L. Maier in *Christianity Today*,

> *The publicity-conscious group of scholars known as the Jesus Seminar now declares that all passages in the Gospels that claim the Jews were at least partly responsible for the Crucifixion are not authentic and should be removed from the New Testament.*[3]

Maier continued:

> *Such revisionism reached a new extreme at a conference held at Oxford in September of 1989, when A. Roy Eckardt, emeritus professor at Lehigh University in Pennsylvania, suggested that Christians ought to abandon the resurrection of Jesus, since it "remains a primordial and unceasing source of the Christian world's anti-Judaism."*[4]

Jim Carroll, author of the best-selling book *Constantine's Sword: The Church and the Jews*, said, "Christianity would never rid itself of the culture and sin of anti-Semitism until its scriptures were newly understood by all Christians as documents corrupted by the human failings of their authors."[5]

It's not hard to figure out how this perception arose. Matthew 23 records Jesus calling the Jewish scribes and Pharisees "hypocrites," "blind guides," "sons of them who killed the prophets," "serpents," "vipers," and saying they cannot "escape the damnation of hell."

Matthew 27:25 states that the Jewish crowd agreed to have responsibility for Jesus' blood placed on them and their children. John 8:44 records Jesus telling the Pharisees, "Ye are of your father the devil," who is described as a liar and a "murderer from the beginning."

By implication then, many would say Jesus taught that all Jews are hypocrites, blind guides, murderers, and liars and that Satan is their father. This perception of New Testament teaching has instilled a strong defensive posture within the Jewish community.

In light of that perception, it is no surprise that an April 22, 2001, article in *The New York Times Magazine* featuring the New York Knicks basketball team created a considerable disturbance. "The Knicks' Dysfunctional Family," was written by Eric Konigsberg, a Jewish journalist who spent time on and off the court with the team, including participating in Bible studies attended by various team members.

In one such study, Charlie Ward and Allan Houston, two prominent players, had a verbal exchange with Konigsberg involving specific New Testament passages. Ward said, "Jews are stubborn. But tell me, why did they persecute Jesus unless he knew something they didn't want to accept? They [the Jews] had his blood on their hands."[6] Houston then turned to Matthew 26:67, which states, "they spat in his [Jesus'] face, and buffeted him; and others smote him with the palms of their hands."

This exchange, which appeared at the end of the article, hit the streets with a bang. The negative reaction spread far beyond the people of New York City. In fact, these players received bad press across the country. The accusations against them were legion. They were described as "bigoted," "racist," and "filled with hate." Ward and Houston simply used the words of the New Testament. Does that mean their accusers were correct? Were Ward and Houston's words anti-Semitic?

A Jewish man named Avi Lipkin insists that the New Testament is not anti-Semitic. "Jewish people ought to read the New Testament," he said. "I tell all my Jewish friends they ought to read the New Testament; and their response to me is, 'What are you? A "Jew for Jesus?"' I answer no, but if you read the New Testament for yourself, you will find out what Christians really believe. They respond by saying, 'Why should we read the New Testament? We don't even read the Old Testament.'"[7]

It is important to understand that regardless of which testament is read, the reading must be done using the golden rule of interpretation:

> When the plain sense of Scripture makes common sense, seek no other sense; therefore, take every word at its primary, ordinary, usual, literal meaning unless the facts of the immediate context studied in the light of related passages and axiomatic and fundamental truths, indicate clearly otherwise.[8]

The director of the Rhea Hirsh School of Education at Hebrew Union College in Los Angeles stated it this way: "It's a Christian moral responsibility not to allow people to come to these texts without context."[9]

Context demands we keep several factors in mind regarding the New Testament. First and foremost is the fact that Jewish people penned most of it. This "Gentile Bible" actually involved Jewish men writing to and about their own people. Its contents almost reads like a debate on the floor of the Knesset (Israeli congress). As one Jewish writer explained, "What people sling back and forth in the Knesset cannot be anti-Jewish, but in Nebraska those would be fighting words."[10]

Consider for a moment the similarity with which Isaiah spoke to his people in the Old Testament:

Ah, sinful nation, a people laden with iniquity, a seed of evildoers, children that are corrupters; they have forsaken the Lord, they have provoked the Holy One of Israel unto anger, they are gone away backward (1:4).

Isaiah, a Jew, was addressing (maybe even yelling at) his fellow Jews.

It is important to note that the centerpiece of the New Testament is Jesus Christ, Yeshua Hamashiach. He was born into a Jewish family in Jewish Bethlehem; celebrated all the Jewish feasts; worshiped in the synagogue; publicly read from the Torah (five books of Moses), the prophets, and the writings; emphasized the Kingdom of God; and preached about the God of Abraham, Isaac, and Jacob. Furthermore, He castigated the leaders who were oppressing their own Jewish people. Also important to the context is the fact that, in the first century when the text was written, the Jewish people were under the authority of the Roman Empire.

If these truths are not understood before the text is read, its message can be severely misunderstood. Consider the first line of the New Testament, found in Matthew: "The book of the genealogy of Jesus Christ, the son of David, the son of Abraham." To fully understand Jesus, we must understand His Jewish roots. Luke, a Gentile, told his readers that Jesus was circumcised on the eighth day (Lk. 2:21). The Jewish apostle John explained that it was on Hanukkah that Jesus declared His deity (Jn. 10:22–30). Acts 22:2–3 records that when Saul (the apostle Paul—not a favorite among Jewish people today) brought his defense "before the people," he spoke in Hebrew and told of his strict Orthodox Jewish upbringing. When James wrote his epistle, he addressed it to the twelve tribes scattered abroad.

It's clear that the New Testament is overwhelmingly Jewish in scope and nature. Yet negative language also is peppered throughout its pages. So, too, is a positive Jewish response to the person and work of Jesus as Messiah. For instance, a great multitude of the daughters of Jerusalem "bewailed and lamented

[Jesus]" (Lk. 23:27). Further, "The word of God increased, and the number of the disciples multiplied in Jerusalem greatly; and a great company of the priests were obedient to the faith" (Acts 6:7). The first church was made up of Jewish people—all Jewish people—including priests.

When understood contextually, the New Testament does not spur hatred for the Jews. On the contrary, it generates love for them. Rev. Bruce McDonald explained it this way:

> *Our whole roots are Judeo-Christian. I'm a minister, been a minister for thirty years. My heroes are Jewish people: Abraham, Isaac, Jacob, David, Elijah, Moses and obviously the Lord Jesus Christ. We believe the Bible is the word of God, and that what it teaches is truth. . . . It obviously would be a horrific sin to be anti-Semitic. That would be going against the very word of God.*[11]

A number of years ago a rabbi hurled a New Testament across a room after he found one of his fellow teachers reading it. When anti-Semitism swept across his homeland of Hungary, he was surprised that, in the name of Christianity, a number of men denounced the anti-Semites and defended the Jewish people. He was amazed. As a result, he started to read the New Testament. He recorded his experience:

> *I had thought the New Testament to be impure, a source of pride, of overweening selfishness, of hatred, of the worst kind of violence. But as I opened it, I felt myself peculiarly and wonderfully taken possession of. A sudden glory, a light, flashed through my soul. I looked for thorns and gathered roses, I discovered pearls instead of pebbles, instead of hatred, love; instead of vengeance, forgiveness; instead of bondage, freedom; instead of pride, humility; instead of enmity, conciliation; instead of death, life, salvation, resurrection, heavenly treasure.*[12]

My perception of the New Testament came from what people told me about it. That view changed dramatically when, shortly after graduation, I not only touched a New Testament for the first time, I read it. I found that this *goyishe* (Gentile) book was as Jewish as my own Holy Scriptures. Gentiles I met who took its contents seriously possessed a genuine love for Jewish people and the Jewish Messiah. One of them, a wonderful Christian gentleman, puts it this way whenever he meets someone Jewish: "What a privilege to meet you. You know, one day I met a Jew; and he changed my life. I've never been the same. I thank God for the Jewish people." He met that Jewish man in the New Testament. His name is Jesus.

WHO KILLED JESUS?

PICTURE THIS: A JEWISH FAMILY SPENDING quality time decorating a Christmas tree. Does this sound odd to you?

When I was 17, I was invited to a Christmas tree decorating party at the home of a Jewish acquaintance. Confusion would best describe my initial reaction to the invitation, followed shortly thereafter by contempt and hostility. I could not understand how a Jewish person could do such a thing.

As I pulled into the driveway, the green pine tree became visible through the open drapes of a huge picture window. As I walked into the house, I saw many of my friends, most of them Jewish, smiling and laughing. I was not amused. It did not take me long to ask the hostess why they, being Jewish, were doing such a thing. The answer floored me. "My dad's company doesn't know that we're Jewish. If they did, he probably wouldn't be working there." She went on to explain that her father was trained as an engineer. At that time, there weren't many Jewish engineers, at least not in his company. He felt that in order to be hired, he had to change his last name to a common Gentile name and let people assume he was a Gentile. Decorating the Christmas tree was part of the charade because her father's boss passed their home to and from work. Her explanation was no joke; she was quite serious. "Let's face it," she said, "to them we are nothing more than Christ killers."

That incident took place almost thirty years ago, and while it is perhaps not typical in America, it would not shock most Jewish people. I believe, however, that it might surprise many Bible-believing Christians. I am often asked in churches, "Why don't the Jewish people accept Jesus as their Messiah?" The people who ask that question usually are motivated by a sincere desire to know. After all, they reason, the prophecies are so clear; Jesus was Jewish; His followers were Jewish; and the New Testament was largely, if not entirely, Jewish. Why wouldn't they believe? It would be a natural. My answer to them is in the form of a question: "Why do any Jewish people believe?"

This brings up another misconception—this time on the part of many Jewish people. It is a common understanding among Jewish people that all Gentiles are Christians, including the Crusaders and Hitler.

For two millennia, the Jewish people have been falsely accused by Gentiles, perhaps professing Christians, of countless horrible acts. In the Middle Ages, we were accused of starting the black plague. The "church" accused us of being a vile and dirty people who were, by our very nature, demonic. They argued strongly that the Passover commemoration was celebrated by drinking the blood of little children. Some even believed, as we have seen, that Jewish men had horns on their heads and hid them with head coverings. Prominent churchmen encouraged book burnings and synagogue demolitions. During the Crusades (1096), soldiers were heard commanding Jewish people to "embrace the cross or die." While seeking to expunge the infidels (Muslims) from the Holy Land, the Crusaders believed it to be a spiritual bonus to terrorize, torture, and kill Jews.

In 1492, when Columbus "sailed the ocean blue," being Jewish in Spain was hazardous to one's health. Forced conversion was the only option for those who wished to remain and live in their beloved country. These kinds of things were carried over into pogroms in Russia and the Holocaust in Hitler's Germany. To this day, being Jewish can be hazardous to one's health. Almost every Jewish person is keenly aware that, like my friend of years ago, "we are nothing more than Christ killers." For them, believing in Christ conjures up thoughts of all the atrocities committed in the name of Christ. Why would any Jew want to be associated with this bloody legacy?

Thankfully, recent years have brought both personal and denominational disclaimers, trying to make amends. The stigma of Christ's dying at the hands of the Jews has even been removed from most official church documents. Yet centuries of diatribes against the Jewish people are not wiped clean by a few years of official changes on paper. The question concerning the death of Christ is a serious issue for Jews and Christians alike. It must not be answered in a politically correct fashion but, rather, in a frank, forthright, and truthful manner.

The essence of the Christian message is found in the simple yet sublime Christian hymn, "Because He Lives." It begins, "God sent His Son, they called Him Jesus, He came to love, heal, and forgive." Jesus the Messiah lives! Death could not stop Him, and the grave could not hold Him. He conquered sin and death by journeying from heaven to earth and taking on Himself the sins of individuals—past, present, and future. Who was responsible for His death? "Wasn't it a Jewish crowd that cried out, 'Crucify him! Crucify him!'?" one might ask. Yes, that is absolutely true, and it is recorded as such in Luke 23:21. But that is only one third of the answer.

The second part of the answer identifies the people who drove those spikes into the Lord's hands and feet. It was, in fact, the Romans who performed that task. It was against Roman law for the Jewish people to carry out capital punishment. Incidentally, doesn't it seem odd that people don't call the Italians Christ killers?

The third part of the answer is the most important. In John 10:17–18 Jesus said, "I lay down my life, that I might take it again. No man taketh it from me, but I lay it down of myself. I have power to lay it down, and I have power to take it again." Hebrews 9:14 states, "the blood of Christ, who through the eternal Spirit offered himself without spot to God . . ."

If history is based on people's opinions rather than on facts gleaned from proper sources, it is no longer true history but *bobbe-myseh* (wives' tales). To say that the Jewish people killed Christ is correct only within the context that all people were responsible. Jewish people may have cried out for His death, but the Gentiles, who could have stopped it, willingly carried it out. Jesus died because that was the only way to satisfy a holy God for the sin that was a part of humanity. He willingly offered Himself for us. He did not have to do it.

Just five years after the Christmas tree decorating incident, I encountered something that seemed just as odd to me, but in an entirely different way. I encountered Gentiles—born-again Gentiles—meeting together with Jewish people to study the Bible. These Christians genuinely loved the Jewish people. They wanted to learn about Passover, Hanukkah, and Sukkot. They understood that their Christian heritage is linked directly to the Jewish people. They understood that the Jews did not put Christ on the cross, nor did the Romans. Rather, it was their own sin—the sin of mankind—that put Him there. And, in His great love for His creation, He gave up His own life to save us all.

JEWISH HUMOR

THE OBSTETRICIAN WANTED TO BE SURE. His patient had told him the date she expected her baby to be born. Taking into account her age, size, and weight gain, the doctor felt it prudent to get more accurate information. "Report to the radiologist for an ultrasound," he told her. "Then we'll see what's what."

So accompanied by her husband, she reported to the radiologist. During the procedure the technician asked, "Why did the doctor have you come here?" The woman explained the reasons.

Meanwhile, the husband was occupying himself by looking at the little screen filled with indiscernible images. The technician calmly pointed out a blinking light that indicated the beating heart of the unborn baby. Then suddenly, without warning, the technician blurted out, "There are two babies here!"

The couple shouted back, "Two babies!" The mother burst into tears, and the father laughed hysterically.

I know the story well, because I am the father of those two babies. My reaction to the announcement of my twins those many years ago was probably similar to that of Abraham's wife, Sarah, thousands of years earlier. At that time she had heard the prophecy that she would bear a son (Gen. 18). She certainly must have said to herself, "at *my* age, from a husband as *old* as my Abraham?" Her reaction, like mine, was to laugh in disbelief. But it was not a joke, and a year later she named her newborn son Isaac, which means "laughter" in Hebrew—a clear reminder of his miracle conception. Interesting that one of our revered patriarchs was named Laughter.

It has been said that comedy is contrived; humor is lived. Humor can unquestionably relieve tension and stress. No doubt, that is why Abraham's wife and I both laughed, demonstrating God's wonderful gift of humor.

Webster's Dictionary defines *humor* as "something that is, or is designed to be, comical or amusing, that quality which appeals to a sense of the ludicrous or absurdly incongruous." In that context, God's Word is filled with humor. In fact, the Hebrew Bible mentions laughter (*zehok*) fifty times.[1] Depending upon the context, the word is translated as "play, enjoy, insult, mock, rejoice," and "scoff."

One cannot help but laugh when picturing the account of the prophet Elijah's meeting with the false prophets of Baal in 1 Kings 18:27. Elijah shouts to them, "Cry aloud; for he is a god. Either he is talking, or he is pursuing, or he is in a journey, or, perhaps, he sleepeth, and must be awakened." Today we could rephrase that something like this: "Why isn't your god doing anything? Oh, I get it. He's on the phone. Or maybe he's on vacation!"

Equally as comical is the narrative in Numbers 22:28: "And the LORD opened the mouth of the ass, and she said unto Balaam, What have I done unto thee, that thou hast smitten me these three times?" Even funnier is the next verse. Balaam answers her!

Consider these from the book of Proverbs: "As a jewel of gold in a swine's snout, so is a fair woman who is without discretion" (11:22); "It is better to dwell in a corner of the housetop, than with a brawling woman in a wide house" (21:9); "It is better to dwell in the wilderness, than with a contentious and an angry woman" (21:19); "A slothful man hideth his hand in his dish, and will not so much as bring it to his mouth again" (19:24); "The slothful man saith, There is a lion outside; I shall be slain in the streets" (22:13).

Clearly, God has stamped His sense of humor within the pages of His Word. And it is just as clear that He has infused it into His Chosen People as well. Jewish humor takes the definition of *humor* and narrows it to something comical or amusing created by Jews, about Jews, and reflecting the lives of Jews. In fact, the amusing verses from Proverbs clearly constitute Jewish humor, encompassing all three of these characteristics.

In *The Big Book of Jewish Humor*, editors William Novak and Moshe Waldoks define a Jewish joke as "one that no goy [Gentile] can understand and every Jew says he has already heard." As an example, they offer this old, yet timeless tidbit: "They say that when you tell a joke to a peasant, he laughs three times—once when you tell the joke, again when you explain it, and yet again when he understands it, for the peasants love to laugh.

"When you tell a joke to a landowner, he laughs twice—once when you tell him the joke, and again when you explain it, for he never really understands it.

"When you tell a joke to an army officer, he laughs only once—when you tell it. He never lets you explain it, and it goes without saying that he is unable to understand it.

"But when you tell a joke to a Jew—even before you've had a chance to finish it, he's already interrupting you. First, he's heard it before. Second, why are you telling it wrong? So he decides to tell you the joke—but in a much better version than yours."[2]

Jewish humor is always *about* something. That something can be food, business, family, anti-Semitism, health, wealth, or survival. Here are some examples: An elderly Jewish man is struck by a car and brought to the hospital. A pretty nurse tucks him into bed and asks, "Mr. Shapiro, are you comfortable?"

Shapiro replies, "I make a nice living."

A Jewish boy comes home from school and tells his mother he's been given a part in the school play. "Wonderful!" she says. "What part is it?"

The boy says, "I play the part of the Jewish husband."

The mother scowls and says, "Go back and tell the teacher you want a speaking part."

Jewish humor is often quick and biting. You can easily miss it if you're not really listening. What did the waiter ask the group of dining Jewish mothers? "Is anything all right?"

A man who dies asks that his ashes be scattered over Bloomingdale's so that his wife will visit once in a while.

It can be sarcastic, complaining, resigned, or descriptive. "Sam, please close the window. It's cold outside."

Sam says, "So, and if I close the window, will it be warm outside?"

A classified ad reads, "Orthodox psychologist who knows how to live well, seeks woman to share bleeding ulcer."[3]

Sometimes the point of the humor is more powerful than the laugh it might deliver. In fact, the appropriate response might not be laughter at all. Instead, a simple nod or a sigh is all that is needed. Cohen and Katz used to play cards every day in a coffeehouse. One day they quarreled and Katz called out, "What kind of guy can you be if you sit down every day to play cards with a guy who sits down to play cards with a guy like you?"

Dr. Avner Ziv is chairman of the Tel Aviv University Department of Educational Sciences in Tel Aviv, Israel. In 1986 he chaired a conference that was attended by academics and comedians to examine Jewish humor. Dr. Ziv made this statement: "Jews, with their long history of pogroms, persecutions and killings, have developed a sense of humor known around the world—that is one of the few positive stereotypes about us."[4]

Indeed, just as Jewish music often takes a minor key—a reminder of the suffering that has framed the Jewish experience—so Jewish humor uses quick wit, self-deprecation, mocking, and biting sarcasm to cope with a seemingly ever-present heartache.

Shalom Aleichem (1859–1916) was inarguably the greatest humorist in all of Jewish literature. His most famous of writings was used to bring to Broadway and to the big screen the bitter-sweet musical *Fiddler on the Roof*. In an early scene, the Jews gather around their beloved rabbi in the village of Ana Tevka. "Rabbi," one of the citizens cries, "is there a proper blessing for the Czar?"

The rabbi strokes his beard and responds, "May God bless and keep the Czar—far away from us!"

This kind of writing epitomized the Talmudic dictum, "Tears of sadness are bad tears, tears of laughter are beautiful" (Shab. 151b–152a). They depict the hard life the Jewish people have had to live.

The works of Shalom Aleichem, more than any other, epitomize the Jewish people's desire to survive. He depicted Jewish society during a time of transition—a time between the old style of Eastern Europe and the advent into modern culture. He communicated with uncanny ability the Jewish struggle just to live and the incredible ability of the Jewish people to adapt to the new situations forced upon them. His characters faced death, shattered dreams, madness, and disintegration. Yet he always countered these tragedies of life with enthusiasm and humor.[5]

Tevye the milkman, in the *Fiddler* story, talks to God on many occasions. He wonders why he is not rich, noting, "It is no shame to be poor. But it's no great honor either!" In another situation, he makes this comment to God, "You help complete strangers— why not me?"

The freedom and opportunity found in America made life for the Jews much easier than the old days of Europe. Jewish humor rose in prominence as Jewish people from New York cooled themselves in the summer in what became known as the "borsht belt" of the Catskill and Pocono Mountains. Jewish people laughed at themselves as they identified with the hilarious tales told masterfully by a generation of Jewish storytellers. It was here that comedians like Sid Caesar and Danny Kaye honed their skills so well that their names became known both in Jewish and Gentile households around the country.

Other well-known Jewish comedians, such as Jack Benny, George Burns, Alan King, and the Marx brothers, built their reputations by relating common, everyday situations in such a way as to elicit a smile and a laugh.

Jewish people have made it so easy for us to laugh at ourselves. And they certainly have shown they can laugh at themselves as well.

Yet as funny as those stories and jokes might be, they are only funny—or even acceptable, for that matter—when told by a person of the same background. Please, if you are not Jewish, don't tell your Jewish friend a demeaning "Jewish joke." It may be funny coming from a Jewish person, but it can be extremely offensive coming from a non-Jewish person.

In her book *Bar Mitzvah*, Sarah Silberstein Swartz says, "It is said that true Jewish humor mirrors the history of the Jewish people—their joys and tragedies, their aspirations and discouragements, their values."[6] Sometimes things hurt so much we just have to laugh. Perhaps that is why God says in His Book, the Bible, that "A merry heart doeth good like a medicine" (Prov. 17:22). And I think that is a good thing.

JEWISH MUSIC—
CAPTURING THE HEART OF A PEOPLE

AS AN ART FORM, MUSIC IS MULTIFUNCTIONAL. It can tell stories, teach, record great events, inspire people to action, vent human emotion, or just be enjoyed. Stated simply, music can capture the heart of a people. It is no wonder that universities offer courses that examine the music and songs of various nationalities.

Most people are familiar with names like Yitzhak Perlman, Yasha Heifitz, Paul Simon and Art Garfunkel, Al Jolson, Victor Borge, and Isaac Stern. They are but a few of the many talented Jewish people who have created listening pleasure for millions across the globe. In fact, Jewish people have contributed immensely to the field of music in a way that is totally disproportionate to their few numbers in the world.

Yet a distinction must be made between Jewish musicians and Jewish music. Jewish music is a legitimate category in the field of musicology. It has been defined as "that music which is made by Jews, for Jews, as Jews."[1] And a grasp of Jewish music provides a marvelous insight into the history, culture, and customs of the Jewish people.

The foundations of Jewish music are entrenched in the Bible. Jewish music began as sacred music created for and centered on the God of Abraham, Isaac, and Jacob. Much of it was performed around the holy Temple. Later it spread to the synagogues and then mushroomed into a wide variety of expressions, largely due to the scattering of the Jewish people around the world, known as the Diaspora.

Not much is known today about the musical arrangements of biblical music. However, the Bible does name specific, individual musical instruments: "The shophar, or ram's horn, is the most frequently mentioned biblical instrument, and the only ancient instrument still in use in the synagogue."[2] Other instruments mentioned include the harp, lyre, flute, tambourine, cymbals, and bells.

The Bible's chief contribution to helping us understand its music lies in the words it provides for various songs. Inherent in these songs are at least three important characteristics: They were written and performed with great *skill*, they exhibited *purpose*, and they enhanced *worship*.

SKILL

It was King David, "the sweet psalmist of Israel" (2 Sam. 23:1) and a skillful musician, who insisted on proficiency for anyone playing music. In Psalm 33:3 he issued this command concerning any new song: "Play skillfully with a loud noise." It might have been David who chose Chenaniah, the leader of the Levites, because Chenaniah was skillful in song. Chenaniah had the ability to lead by giving instructions concerning a song sung during the procession of the Ark of the Covenant (1 Chr. 15:22).

It was David who organized the musicians into "courses" and instructed the leaders of the Levites to appoint musicians to perform as the Ark of the Covenant was moved from Obed-edom's home to its proper place in Jerusalem (1 Chr. 15:16). These Levites "were instructed in the songs of the LORD, even all that were skillful" (1 Chr. 25:7). In all, 288 skillful men sang and/or played various instruments (1 Chr. 25:7).

It seems that under David's leadership, good music was the rule rather than the exception. This fact is evidenced in the prophet Ezekiel's observation that people come to God with the "lovely song of one that hath a pleasant voice, and can play well on an instrument" (Ezek. 33:32). Skillfully played music was a part of Jewish life.

Psalms 120—134 are called the Psalms of Ascents, or songs of degrees. Differing views exist as to when these psalms were sung. The first view holds that Jewish people sang them as they ascended up to Jerusalem for required worship there on Passover, Pentecost, and Tabernacles (Dt. 16:16). A second view states that they were sung while worshipers stood on the fifteen steps leading to the Court of Israel in the Temple.[3] Regardless of which view is correct, these "songs" were written and performed with the skill and precision needed to provide the proper rhythm of the ascent.

There are seventy-one instances where the word *selah* is used. The word *selah* was not actually spoken but was used as "a musical notation signaling an interlude or change of musical accompaniment."[4] Fifty-five of the psalms employ a chief musician or choir director, suggesting "that a collection of psalms existed for the choir director, possibly for use on special occasions."[5] Even a casual Bible reader can see that music was important enough to be performed skillfully.

PURPOSE

In the Torah, God commanded Moses to write a song and teach it to the children of Israel (Dt. 31:19). The song's purpose, found in Deuteronomy 32, was to remind the Israelites of the unique place they hold under the watchful eye of the God of Abraham, Isaac, and Jacob. It also serves as a tool to teach Jewish history to future generations.

In addition to songs of remembrance and instruction, songs in the Bible were written for other purposes. They were sung to celebrate great victories, such as the one recorded in Exodus 15 and sung by Moses, Miriam, and the children of Israel. The song of Deborah and Barak, recorded in Judges 5, describes the Israelite victory over the army of Jabin.

"Such heroic ballads," said one scholar, "were probably set down in the lost 'Book of the Wars of the Lord' (Num. 21:14) and the 'Book of Jashar' (Josh. 10:13; 2 Sam. 1:18), and were no doubt sung by itinerant minstrels and bards."[6] The song recorded in 2 Samuel 1:19–27 expresses David's great sadness as he mourns the loss of Saul and his beloved friend, Jonathan.

Excessive drinking is denounced in Psalm 69:12. Psalm 30 was written and performed for the dedication of the house of David. Love songs are found throughout the poetic books of the Holy Scriptures—1,005 of them written by Solomon alone (1 Ki. 4:32). Many songs were sung about the great city of Zion. Psalm 137 explains that these songs became hard to sing. An unnamed composer wrote the following:

> By the rivers of Babylon, there we sat down, yea, we wept, when we remembered Zion. We hung our harps upon the willows in the midst thereof. For there they that carried us away captive required of us a song; and they that wasted us required of us mirth, saying, Sing us one of the songs of Zion. How shall we sing the LORD's song in a foreign land? (vv. 1–4).

To ensure that Israel's beloved Jerusalem would be remembered, he continued, "If I forget thee, O Jerusalem, let my right hand forget her cunning. If I do not remember thee, let my tongue cleave to the roof of my mouth, if I prefer not Jerusalem above my chief joy" (vv. 5–6). We know that life's situations can turn songs of joy into songs of lament (Amos 8:10).

Hallelujah songs were written simply to praise the Lord. No better example of this purpose exists than Psalm 150, which tells us where to praise Him, how to praise Him, who should praise Him, and what to praise Him for.

WORSHIP

Worship is as much an attitude as it is an action. The Hebrew word *shachah* is translated "to bow down," "to depress," and "to prostrate oneself." This is a posture long associated with the Jewish people. When implemented, it communicates reverence as well as the homage due to the Sovereign One of the universe. Many songs in Jewish Scripture capture that attitude. First Chronicles 16:37–43 tells us how the Levites behaved before the Ark of the Covenant. They offered continual burnt offerings and expressions of thanksgiving. Musical instruments played the "songs of God" (v. 42; cf. 2 Chr. 7:6; 29:25). How amazing that must have been to behold!

The hallelujah psalms (the word *psalm* comes from the Greek translation of the Hebrew word *mizmor*[7]) are songs accompanied by instruments used to shower the Lord with musical praise. First Chronicles 6:31–32 records that David set people "over the service of song in the house of the LORD, after the ark had rest. And they ministered before the dwelling place of the tabernacle of the congregation with singing."

When Nehemiah led the people to rebuild the walls of Jerusalem, "all Israel, in the days of Zerubbabel, and in the days of Nehemiah, gave the portions of the singers and the porters, every day its portion; and they sanctified holy things unto the Levites, and the Levites sanctified them unto the children of Aaron" (Neh. 12:47). This was music arranged with worship in mind.

This kind of Jewish music is the basis for heavenly music. We find such music described in the last book of the New Testament. In Revelation 5:9 we read, "And they sang a new song, saying, Thou art worthy to take the scroll, and to open its seals; for thou wast slain, and hast redeemed us to God by thy blood out of every kindred, and tongue, and people, and nation." According to verse 8, this song was sung to the accompaniment of harps.

A great deal of controversy embroils the evangelical community today about the type of music we use in worship, the way it is performed, and the volume at which it is played.

I do not intend to address that topic here. It is, however a valuable exercise to examine truths about biblical music directly from the pages of Scripture. There we see that heaven will be playing some of Earth's songs. (See Revelation 15:3; Exodus 15; and Deuteronomy 32.)

With that in mind, we should follow the Jewish, biblical pattern. As with the children of Israel, our music ministries should be performed with great skill and to the best of the abilities God has given us. Our music should exhibit purpose, containing a real message. Finally, our music should enhance worship by directing those who sing it or hear it to the throne of God. After all, that is something we will be doing for all eternity.

In Old Testament days, Jewish worship revolved first around the Tabernacle and later the Temple. Crucial to that worship was music, particularly the skill and purpose of its presentation. In accordance with 2 Chronicles 29:25–27, the priests from the tribe of Levi were directed to play various instruments skillfully as biblical psalms were performed.

In A.D. 70 a stunning event dramatically altered Jewish life. The Romans attacked Jerusalem, leveled the Temple, and forced the city's mostly Jewish population to flee. This action ended sacrifices, stopped all Levitical activity, and silenced the music. As a result, the rabbis forbade the playing of all music, believing that only a total ban could adequately express the tremendous grief associated with the Temple's destruction.

Not all Jewish people, however, embraced the decision. The issue eventually came before the great Jewish sage Maimonides, who issued this simple and logical ruling: "In spite of the rigor of the law, music could not be suppressed."[8] By the third century A.D., the ban on all music had become largely disregarded. Yet it was upheld in the synagogue and extends even to this day in the Orthodox tradition.

Observant Jewish people believe music will resume when Messiah comes, the Temple is rebuilt, and Temple worship restored. One unique "instrument," however, has never left the synagogue. This quintessential Jewish instrument is the shofar, or ram's horn. Some people even believe the sound of the shofar "possesses strength and powers beyond that of common instruments."[9] It is the one instrument played in times ranging from great joy to great despair. Its sound is compulsory during Rosh Hashanah (New Year) and Yom Kippur (Day of Atonement) services.

As global wanderers, the Jewish people have been able to preserve their identity while incorporating into it many of the foreign cultural elements into which they migrated. Thus, to understand what makes music uniquely Jewish, it is probably best to explore three basic categories—religious, celebratory, and entertaining—and three primary styles—Ashkenazi, Sephardi, and Mizrahi.

Ashkenazi originated in such Eastern European countries as Romania and Bulgaria, then extended west and north and eventually reached America. The primary language used is Yiddish (a Hebrew/German mixture). Sephardi originated in countries along the Mediterranean, such as Spain, Morocco, and Turkey. The primary language for this music is Ladino, a mixture of Hebrew and Spanish. And Mizrahi, which means "east," is Arabic in style, originating in such countries as Persia, Iraq, and Egypt. Its primary language is Hebrew.

MELODIES TO DRAW THE HEART

Because only a capella music was allowed at Jewish religious services, a melodious chant arose that is still employed today. Rabbi Judah he-Hasid (1150–1217) said, "Say your prayers in a melody that is most pleasant and sweet to you . . . because the melody will draw your heart after the words that come from your mouth. Supplicate in a melody that makes the heart weep, praise in a melody that makes the heart glad."[10]

The Talmud, Judaism's all-important, extrabiblical work, exhorts, even requires, a worship leader to be "skilled in chanting and having a pleasant voice."[11] Some special melodies are memorized and passed down from generation to generation. Incorporated with scriptural texts, these are called *cantillations.*

Cantillations are "vocal inflections used for emphasis while reading texts aloud, inflections which were handed down by oral tradition until the 10th century, when they were codified."[12] The reader chants the text using only a series of musical notations that look like squiggles above or below each word. These are called *trop.* Said one expert, "Christian Gregorian chanting is actually a descendant of Jewish chanting of the Torah via cantillation."[13]

Any Jewish boy preparing to become a bar mitzvah is familiar with these marks. His responsibility is to memorize the musical voice inflections associated with each little mark and then memorize his *haftorah,* the portion of Scripture read on his special day. On the day of his bar mitzvah, he marries the marks with the text in the prescribed singsong manner.

Cantillations are taught in *yeshivot* (Hebrew schools) or by a tutor. Depending on the Scripture, they are sung either in a melancholy or happy tune. Either way, they were recorded as "musical notations . . . which have served as accents, punctuation marks, and musical interpretations of the texts."[14]

In addition to scriptural voice music, prayers known as *nusaim* are also chanted. Recited on the high holidays and festivals, some of these chants go as far back as the days of the ancient Temples:

> *These simple responsive and unison readings in the
> Temple gave rise to the ancient synagogue melodies
> which became the core of the synagogue* Nusah, *as
> we read in the Talmud: "At the time the Israelites
> ascended from the Red Sea . . . how did they render
> the song [of Moses]? . . . R. Nehemiah declares:
> Like a school-teacher who recites the* Shema *in the*

synagogue, viz., he begins first and they respond
after him. (Sotah 30b).[15]

Not every prayer has or had a distinctive *nusah*. Over time
new *nusaim* have been introduced. Usually the person who
writes these new prayers is the *hazan*, or cantor. Today a cantor
must have a professional quality voice that adds a powerful
dimension to the service, as well as the ability to write musical
prayers. Whether Orthodox, Conservative, or Reform, every
synagogue usually employs a full-time cantor. In many
instances, cantors write *nusaim* continually. It should be noted
that, while Orthodox Jews continue to abide by the ban on
instruments and choirs, most Conservative and Reform congregations do not. For these two groups, the quality of the music
takes precedence over the performer's piety or religious background. Thus some congregations hire Gentiles to sing their
worship songs.

Hasidism, the most pious of all Jewish movements, roots its
worship in the concept of joy. This thrust reflects the teaching of
its founder, an 18th-century Eastern European mystic named
Israel Ben Eliezer, known throughout Judaism as *Baal Shem Tov*
("Master of the Good Name"). Said one Jewish author, "The
ecstasy of melody is one of the primary keys that Hasidism used
to unlock the gates of heaven. It is, so to speak, the ladder to the
throne of God."[16]

The words to Hasidic music are among the easiest to recite.
They are words like *la-la, bim-bam-bim, vim-va-voom, dai-dai-dai,*
etc. In the movie *Fiddler on the Roof,* Tevya the milkman sang the
song "If I Were a Rich Man," using many such words.

A Hasidic rabbi once said that melody is the outpouring of
emotions. Thus the tunes and, in many cases, the words spring
from the heart. One of the best-known Hasidic melodies is not
even known as Hasidic at all. Regarded as an Israeli song, it is
played at most Jewish weddings and bar mitzvahs around the
world. Performed by many well-known recording artists, it was
created "in the court of the rebbe of Sadigura at the turn of the

century."[17] The words are simple: "Come let us be glad and rejoice. Come sing and be gay. Awake brothers with a joyful heart." The tune is electric. When people hear it, they are captivated and inspired to sing it, dance, and clap their hands. Perhaps you will recognize it as *Hava Nagilah*. Hasidim also uses dance in its music and worship. From the gentle sway while praying, to the vigorous dance of the *hora*, Hasidism teaches that the whole being must be able to sing. This belief is based on Psalm 35:10: "All my bones shall say, LORD, who is like unto thee . . . ?" Some of these dances are still used today.

MELODIES TO GROW OLD WITH

Celebratory and entertaining music take into account life-cycle events, such as bar mitzvahs, weddings, and anniversaries. These types of music are pleasant to listen to, and both instruments and voice are used frequently. Probably the two most popular instruments with Jewish people are the violin and clarinet. "Why this should be so, no one really knows, though there's a joke that says: 'Have you already seen someone running away from a pogrom [persecution] with a piano under his arm?'"[18]

A particular style of music that many people identify as Jewish is *klezmer*. Yet, according to klezmer expert Ari Davidow, "Not all Jewish musicians play klezmer, not all Jewish music is klezmer, and not all klezmorim [people who play klezmer] are Jewish."[19] Larry Maxey, a non-Jewish clarinetist, called klezmer "a microcosm of all that music has to offer—joy, pathos, dance, lyricism."[20]

The word *klezmer* is Yiddish but comes from the biblical Hebrew *kley zemer* or *kelizemer*, meaning "vessels of song."[21] Describing klezmer music is difficult. Bands play it; yet drums, common to most bands, usually do not. A pure klezmer band is not supposed to have vocalists, yet many do.

Klezmer music had its beginnings in the fifteenth century in the *shtetls*, the close-knit, Yiddish-speaking communities of

Eastern Europe; yet it thrives today in the musical meccas of America. Klezmer bands don't limit themselves to klezmer music and usually play anything from Israeli tunes to jazz to rock 'n' roll.

Klezmer music was designed to dance to. It swings. What jazz is to the African-American community, klezmer is to the Jewish community. Some people would even call it Jewish soul music. Said writer Moshe Denburg,

> *The Jewish people and their music have their roots in the Middle East, specifically in the land of Israel, and their branches everywhere. They have lived, for over 2000 years, amongst many cultures, both Eastern and Western—from Iran to Israel, to the Western Mediterranean and North Africa, to Europe, and most recently, the Americas.*[22]

Their love for music can be seen by looking at the number of their accomplished musicians. If you check the list of musicians in the *Encyclopaedia Judaica*, you will see eighteen full pages of accomplished composers, instrumentalists, musicologists, singers, writers, and conductors. It is no accident that one of the all-time favorite songs in Israel is called, simply, "Hallelujah." God has blessed the world with the wonderful ability to play and hear music. We can all say or sing Hallelujah—praise the Lord!

FROM BADGE TO BANNER

VEXILLOLOGY. MOST PEOPLE HAVE never heard the term; but according to *World Book Encyclopedia*, it is the study of the history and symbolism of flags. Its root can be traced to the Latin word for "square flag" or "banner"—*vexillum*.

Today every country in the world has a flag uniquely designed to represent it. Usually, careful thought has been invested in choosing just the right colors and emblems to symbolize the national identity, with the hope that just the sight of the flag will inspire, motivate, and encourage the country's citizens.

And generally it does. In America, many of us have been known to wipe away a tear or two each time Old Glory soars into ascendancy during the awards ceremonies at the international Olympics.

The citizens of the modern State of Israel are no different and are unsurpassed in demonstrating emotion and pride in their flag. Simply designed, the Israeli flag incorporates a solid white background overlaid with two horizontal blue stripes. Displayed prominently on this field of white is the blue Star of David. Its thoughtful design inspires people to think beyond their own modern state. It is a flag that binds the people of Israel today with the people of Israel in the time of King David himself. Israel stands as the lone nation in the world whose flag has its roots in the pages of Scripture. In the Hebrew Bible, God communicated His desire for visible rallying points for His people Israel. Two Hebrew words are used to designate that desire: _degel_ and _nes_. _Degel_ is rendered variously as "flag," "banner," or "standard" and was used by Moses in the book of Numbers. _Nes_, translated "ensign" or "banner," was used by the prophets Isaiah and Jeremiah.

Numbers 1:52 records that the children of Israel were to "pitch their tents, . . . every man by his own standard." In addition, they were instructed to encamp "with the banner of their father's house" (Num. 2:2). Each tribe possessed a God-given emblem that distinguished it from the others. This provided orderly movement for a population that was estimated in the millions.

The prophet Isaiah recorded that in the future, Messiah will "set up an ensign for the nations" (Isa. 11:12). In the book of Jeremiah, the word _standard_ indicates a rallying point: "Blow the trumpet . . . Assemble yourselves, . . . Set up the standard toward Zion" (Jer. 4:5–6).

No trace of those flags or banners exists today. Dispersed into cultures extending to the four corners of the earth, the Jewish people were divided for nearly two thousand years, with no homeland in which to raise a banner of national identity. In the early years of Zionism, Theodor Herzl, founder of the modern State of Israel, began thinking that a flag could help unite his cause. On June 12, 1895, he recorded in his diary that he was contemplating a white flag with seven golden stars: white to symbolize the new life that awaited his countrymen in their land, and seven stars to depict the seven working hours in a day.[1]

For the next two years, Herzl and other prominent Zionists dialogued concerning the flag's design; but they could not seem to reach a consensus. According to an article entitled "The

Israeli Flag," cited by The Jewish Student Online Research Center (JSOURCE), David Wolffsohn, a colleague of Herzl's at the First Zionist Congress in Basil, Switzerland, in 1897, said this of its birth:

> What flag would hang in the Congress Hall? Then an idea struck me. We have a flag—and it is blue and white. The talith (prayer shawl) with which we wrap ourselves when we pray: that is our symbol. Let us take this Talith [or tallit] from its bag and unroll it before the eyes of Israel and the eyes of all the nations. So I ordered a blue and white flag with the Shield of David painted upon it.[2]

The blue stripes affixed to Israel's flag serve as a reminder of the attire Jewish men wear when they pray to the God of Abraham, Isaac, and Jacob. Even before the flag was created, a man named L. A. Frankl wrote a poem in 1860 entitled "Zivei Erez Yehudah," describing its colors: "All that is sacred will appear in these colors: white—as the radiance of great faith [and] blue—like the appearance of the firmament."[3] Because the exact shade of blue that was to have been used on the tallit is unknown, the flag has no determined shade either. Thus light blue is used, knowing that no one knows what the correct shade should really be.

The Star of David in the center of the flag has long been regarded as a Jewish symbol. It is often referred to as the "Jewish star" by both Jewish people and Gentiles alike. The star is formed by one triangle superimposed upon another—one pointing up, the other pointing down. According to JSOURCE, "by leading a life of Torah and mitzvot [good deeds] the Jew strives to bring together the worlds of the spiritual [point facing up] and the earthly [point facing down], the worlds of the holy and the secular."[4]

Other interpretations also abound. One is that the six outer points stand for the six aspects of the Lord's spirit: wisdom, understanding, counsel, might, knowledge, and fear of the Lord.

Another contends that the star represents the three aspects of man: body, soul, and spirit.

There is no reference to the Star of David in the Bible. In fact, the Hebrew *Magen David* means "Shield of David" rather than "Star of David." Tradition says that the six-pointed star appeared on David's battle shield, but there is no hard evidence to substantiate that belief. What is known, however, is that the Nazis used the star as a badge of shame, forcing the Jewish people to wear it on their outer clothing to mark them out for persecution and extermination.

The nation of Israel took that badge of shame and turned it, instead, into a bold and striking symbol of pride for Jewish people everywhere.

Although *vexillology* may not be a well-known word, or even a well-known discipline, it is, nevertheless, helpful in understanding the nation of Israel. It would be most beneficial, however, to apply the discipline of vexillology to *Jehovah-nis'si*, ("the LORD is my banner" [Ex. 17:15]). Doing that might yield more than historical information—it might yield a relationship with the true and living God.

BAPTISM OR MIKVEH?

"STEVE, I CAN'T DO IT, I JUST CAN'T do it. I know all about the plans we've made, but this is not going to happen. I'm Jewish; this would be too much for my family." The voice on the other end of the phone was quivering with emotion. This was not the Mike I knew. Usually he was self-assured, confident, and strong. On the phone he sounded frightened and intimidated.

Mike and I had met through a mutual friend and immediately struck up a friendship. Over time he and his wife became interested in spiritual things and began attending our home Bible study. After many meetings and dozens of answered questions, Mike received Jesus as his Messiah. He was so excited! Constantly reading God's Word brought Mike to the inevitable question of baptism. He soon began planning his own private ceremony, with a sensitivity toward his many invited Jewish guests. He really wanted the opportunity to explain to them what had happened in his life. The leadership at a local church agreed to allow the use of their facilities. The date was set, and more than fifty invitations were sent.

His phone call canceling the ceremony came on the very day it was scheduled to occur, just hours before it was to start. What had happened? And why?

Most Gentiles and Christians consider it a privilege to witness or participate in a baptism. This is not the case for Jewish people, however, who view it as taboo for several reasons. First, Jews who are baptized are viewed as *meshumeds*, or *traitors*. In Jewish eyes, they have shamed their families and the Jewish community by forsaking their people, their heritage, and their traditions. Second, baptism speaks to the Jewish person of *forced conversion*, a reminder of the thousands of people over the years who were threatened with the loss of property or life if they refused to undergo it. Baptism is associated with Christianity and is generally viewed as no friend of the Jewish people. The very word *baptism* sends shivers up the spines of many Jewish people.

On the phone Mike told me he had been thinking about what was going to take place. He thought about the effect baptism would have on his family, some of whom had said they were deeply hurt and would never attend such an event. Mike said, "I'm not a traitor, but they think I am. I don't know if I can bear that thought."

Was Mike's family correct? Was he a Jewish man betraying his heritage? What was I to tell him?

Immersion is nothing new to the Jewish people. Its purpose has always been for cleansing, although not physical cleansing. Maimonides, the great Jewish sage, said, "Uncleanness is not mud or filth which water can remove, but is a matter of scriptural decree and dependent on the intention of the heart." Thus, rabbinical thought holds that there must be a special intent for being immersed, or there is no value in the immersion.

During the days of the Tabernacle and Temple, Jewish law required immersion in the event of spiritual uncleanness, such as contact with a dead body (Num. 19) or an emission of unclean bodily fluid (Lev. 15). In A.D. 70, such immersions ceased due to the Roman destruction of the Temple. Other kinds of immersions continued, however.

Today, immersions take place for a variety of reasons. They are carried out in a *mikveh*, "a collection of water." This special pool contains a minimum of 120 gallons of water, the majority of which must be "moving," such as rain, melted snow, or ice. These ritual baths are divided into two sides, one for men and one for women. The "bathers" must first shower, and they then are given white cotton coverings to place on their bodies. They are escorted into the bath, where complete submersion must be achieved.

Orthodox Jews (a minority of the Jewish population) are usually the only ones who use a mikveh today, which is why these baths are primarily located in religious neighborhoods. *Tevilah,* or *immersion,* is used when a person converts to Judaism or in preparation for special days like the Sabbath or the Day of Atonement. Couples about to be married must enter the waters of a mikveh, separately, just before the wedding.

While there are many reasons for a mikveh, it is most often used by married women who have been in a state of separation (*niddah*) from their husbands during their monthly cycle. The Torah demands that couples abstain from marital relations during this time. Before they resume relations, the wife must go into the waters of the mikveh for purification. As the woman immerses herself, she recites two blessings: "Blessed art thou, O Lord our God, King of the Universe, who hast hallowed us with thy commandments and commanded us concerning immersion," and "Blessed art thou, O Lord our God, King of the Universe, who hast kept us in life and sustained us and enabled us to reach this significant moment." Once she has immersed herself, she is ready to come together with her husband.

Regardless of the reason for the immersion, its importance is regarded as internal, not external.

The Gospels tell of a Jewish prophet named John who came out of the wilderness of Judea to preach a message of repentance to his people. He was to prepare them for the Messiah and the coming kingdom, which was at hand. Jewish people from Jerusalem and all of Judea came to him to be immersed in the Jordan River, where they publicly confessed their sins.

Luke records that the people wondered if John himself was, in fact, the Messiah. John responded by saying, "I indeed baptize you with water; but one mightier than I cometh, the latchet of whose shoes I am not worthy to loose" (Lk. 3:16).

These were Jewish people, called by a Jewish prophet, to do a perfectly acceptable and necessary biblical thing—immerse themselves in a body of moving water to publicly express an inward reality. In this case, it was to express sorrow for sin. Remember the rabbinical rule: There must be special intent, or the immersion is useless.

When Jesus arrived, John was reluctant to baptize Him, requesting instead that *Jesus* baptize *him*. He correctly stated that Jesus was greater than he: "He must increase, but I must decrease" (Jn. 3:30). Jesus insisted, however, that John baptize Him. Jesus needed no inward or outward cleansing, but His public baptism was used by God as a significant ceremony to launch His Son's earthly ministry, as well as to introduce Him to and identify Him with His people. This would begin His public and prophetic journey to His death and resurrection.

Followers of Jesus today do not receive baptism because there is something unique or powerful about the water. Without a heart decision, without that "intent of the heart" as described by the rabbis, baptism is just a public show. But when people recognize that they are sinners and that the provision to satisfy a holy God has been met through the person of the Messiah, Jesus, they desire to identify with His death and resurrection.

As Mike and I discussed his decision to halt his baptism, I could sense that something was happening, even as we spoke on the phone. His voice was gaining strength and a sense of confidence. For a few minutes, it seemed that he was speaking, not to me, but to himself. It was almost as if I was not even there. He was actually talking himself into going through with it. He knew this would be his opportunity to explain, in his own words, the very Jewish thing he was doing. He could assure his family and friends that he would never betray his

Jewish heritage, a heritage he was proud of. He could tell them that he loved them and that his only desire was for them to read the Jewish Scriptures, where they, too, could find the Messiah. He could tell them that he understood why this ceremony might cause some pain. As he would stand in that little baptismal pool in a small local church, he could tell them that his decision to receive Christ had brought him peace and joy, and he could explain his decision to everyone at the same time. Just before the conversation ended Mike said, "Steve, we have to do this."

And that is exactly what we did!

Typical Israeli Vegetable Salad.

Try It—You'll Like It!

FOR MANY OF US, EATING IS AN emotional experience. The sights and aromas of various foods evoke wide-ranging passions, both positive and negative. It is not uncommon to observe grimaces and other facial contortions as people taste new or different foods. What a shame that some people are so reluctant to sample unusual fare. If they did, they would probably find that some foods really aren't as bad as they thought. In fact, sampling new dishes can be downright exciting.

In some of my diverse travels, I have had the privilege and opportunity of sampling many different ethnic foods. Eating some of these delicacies has provided me with greater insight into the diversity within the world that God has given us.

Several years ago, I was the guest of some Mexican friends for a genuine Mexican dinner. Grandma Carrera is the family matriarch—mother of eight adult children and grandmother of numerous grandchildren, many of whom were in attendance. We were seated at one long table that extended from the dining room well into the living room. Chairs lined both sides of the table, and the meal was served family style.

I was seated with my wife at one end of the table, while the hostess was at the other end. She seemed to be a mile away. Shortly after the meal began, a commotion erupted on her side of the table. I wondered what the problem was. One of her children explained, "My mother insists that if you are going to eat a real Mexican meal, you must eat all the things we eat."

Now I was really curious. "Great, what do you want me to eat?" I asked.

The response came in the form of a mumble. "Well, it's pickled pig's feet. I told her not to do this, that you are Jewish, and we don't want to offend you."

I thanked her for her sensitivity. It's true, pig's feet are not exactly kosher. However, I understand that Christ made all things clean. Smiling, I signaled to someone to send them down to me. As the bowl of gelatinous white things came into my vision, I could also see heads on both sides of the table lean forward and turn my way. All eyes seemed to be fixed on me. I helped myself to a fork full, accompanied by the sound of low moans. I must confess that I have not had pig's feet since, but eating them set the stage for a wonderful day of fellowship. Since that time many years ago, a lot of Mexican and Jewish food has been shared. Eating those pig's feet was a defining moment.

A similar incident occurred in the home of a Jamaican family who had invited me to lunch after a Sunday morning meeting. Arriving at their home, I immediately felt engulfed in their culture. I loved hearing them all speak with their unique accent. As we sat down to eat, I was informed that the "heat" in the food had been toned down in my honor. "So, what are we having?" I asked.

The answer came swiftly and proudly. "We were able to secure fresh goat."

Fresh Jamaican goat stew! I must say, it was not like anything I had eaten before. It was outstanding.

At yet another Sunday dinner, I dined with an East Indian family. Like the Mexican and Jamaican families, they were gracious and hospitable brothers and sisters in Christ. They were also willing to keep the "heat" to a minimum. I never knew you could use curry in so many dishes. That, too, was delicious.

On each of these occasions, the individuals served food from their native countries. They were proud of who they were and were able to explain their culture simply by serving the food they loved. Each time, serving the food was a labor of love. As I ate what they liked to eat, I was able to learn many things about them. And they, in turn, asked questions about my family and background. We were able to share ethnic cultural differences and learn about one another.

Eating the food of another culture gives us insight into the lives of the people of that culture. Jesus often ate with His disciples. In fact, the last chapter of the Gospel of John relates that the resurrected Jesus fixed breakfast for them as He taught them what love and commitment really are.

If you are interested in learning about the Jewish people, it would help you to taste some of our food. Many people enjoy the different colors, textures, and aromas emanating from the foods our people enjoy. Following are recipes for some of my favorite dishes. I have made sure that none of them contains "heat" to speak of, nor do I ask you to confront a meat product unfamiliar to you. I really would love to prepare these dishes for you, but since I cannot, you will have to step out in faith and give them a try. Some of these dishes I grew up with and consumed on various holidays; others are just part of our culture. After you try these recipes yourself, invite Jewish friends for dinner, and, as you break bread together, you may have the opportunity to bring the bread of life to them. You may want to use kosher ingredients, just to be safe. That would demonstrate sensitivity for your Jewish friend.

Classic Challah or Sabbath Bread is a double-braided, slightly sweet egg bread that reminds the Jewish people that God provided a double portion of manna while they were in the wilderness.

3 tbsp. yeast	1 tbsp. salt
1/3 c. oil	9 c. flour
2 1/4 c. lukewarm water	1/3 c. sugar
4 eggs	

Dissolve yeast in water and let stand for 10 minutes. Add salt, sugar, oil, and eggs. Add flour, 3 cups at a time, beating well after each addition. Knead dough on a lightly floured board for approximately 7 minutes until smooth and elastic, adding flour as necessary, possibly up to 1 cup more. Place in a large greased bowl, turning the dough once so the greased side is on top. Cover with a clean, damp towel and let stand in a warm place to rise for 1 1/2 hours, or until double in bulk. Punch down completely so there are no air pockets. Divide dough into 6 equal portions; shape into ropes about 1" in diameter. Braid 3 ropes together to form a loaf. Repeat for a second loaf. Place on greased cookie sheets. Let rise again until double in size. Brush with glaze and sprinkle with sesame or poppy seeds. Bake at 350° for 30 minutes. Remove to racks to cool.[1]

———◆◆◆———

Mom's Passover Rolls are made without leaven . We used to call them air biscuits. At least they can hold meat for a sandwich.

2/3 c. water	1 c. matzo meal
1/4 tsp. salt	1 tbsp. sugar
1/3 c. oil	3 eggs

Bring the water, oil, sugar, and salt to a boil. Slowly add matzo meal, mixing as you pour. Let cool. Add eggs, beating after each addition. Drop by large spoonfuls onto a greased baking sheet. Bake at 350° for 45–60 minutes.
* These can also be formed into balls with wet hands.

———◆◆◆◆◆———

Chicken Paprikash, a favorite in our home, was passed down from my mother's Hungarian background.

1 cut-up chicken	3 tbsp. tomato paste
2 chicken boullion cubes	paprika
1 onion, chopped	

Brown chicken and onion in oil. After they are browned, add boullion cubes and enough water to cover chicken. Simmer 10–15 minutes, add tomato paste and paprika to taste. Cook 1 to 1 1/2 hours. Serve with noodles or rice.

———◆◆◆◆◆———

Kugel or Noodle Pudding is a side dish, rather than a dessert. It is often served with brisket.

12 oz. noodles	1/2 c. butter, margarine, or
1/4 tsp. salt	schmaltz (chicken fat)
3/4 c. sugar	3/4 c. coarsely chopped
4 eggs, well-beaten	walnuts

Cook noodles as directed; drain well. Add sugar, raisins, nuts, salt, and eggs. Melt fat in baking pan and pour the balance of the fat into the noodle mixture. Blend well and spread mixture in baking pan. Sprinkle evenly with cinnamon. Bake at 375° for 55 minutes or until browned.

———◆◆◆◆◆———

Michele's Brisket is typically served on the Sabbath or other special occasions. This recipe comes from a former neighbor and wonderful cook.

4–5 lbs. first-cut only brisket of beef (or 3–5 lbs. point end)
1 1/2 tbsp. Worcestershire sauce
garlic powder   celery leaves

1 onion   1 beef boullion cube
1/2 c. chili sauce

Rub Worcestershire sauce on both sides of brisket and brown on both sides in skillet. Sprinkle with garlic powder. Place in baking dish with fatty side up. Cut up an onion; lay on brisket. Add celery leaves. Mix chili sauce with 1/4 cup water and pour over onion. Dissolve beef boullion cube in 1/2 cup water. Pour into pan with brisket. Seal baking dish tightly with foil. Bake at 300–325° for 3 1/2 hours. If desired, add peeled and cut-up potatoes after the first hour and a half.

Matzo Balls for Matzo Ball Soup, which is often referred to as "Jewish penicillin." It is to be served in your favorite chicken broth and vegetables—usually onions, celery, and carrots. A definite taste of home and cure-all for what ails you!

2 tbsp. melted fat, butter, or oil   2 tbsp. soup stock or water
1 tsp. salt, if desired   1/2 c. matzo meal
2 large eggs, slightly beaten

Blend fat or oil and eggs together. Mix matzo meal and salt together. Combine these two mixtures and blend well. Add soup stock and mix until uniform. Cover mixing bowl and chill at least 15 minutes. Using 2- or 3-quart pot, bring 1 1/2 quarts of slightly salted water to a brisk boil. Reduce flame and into slightly boiling water drop balls approximately 1" in diameter from chilled mixture. Cover pot and cook 30–40 minutes. With soup at room temperature or warmer, remove matzo balls from water and place into soup pot. When ready to serve, allow soup to simmer about 5 minutes. Recipe makes about 8 matzo balls.

* If you decide to double or triple this recipe, be sure to allow ample water in pot for matzo balls to expand. Otherwise, you'll have cannonballs!

What's In a Name?

ONE OF THE WONDERFUL THINGS about becoming parents is the ongoing debate between husband and wife over what to name the child. What couple hasn't purchased a book of names and then uttered the words, "Hey, what about . . .?" Every generation seems to produce names that become trendy and popular.

When my wife and I were expecting our first child, we held numerous dialogues and sounded out many possibilities. One thing we knew for certain: The name would start with S. Why? Because I had promised my father that my firstborn would be named for his father Shmuel (Samuel), who had died when I was a child.

You see, in the tradition of the Ashkenazic Jews, children are named for the deceased—usually relatives. It is not acceptable to name a child for a living person. According to legend, it is feared that if the name of an older living person is used for a new baby, when it is time for the death angel to come for the older person, he may become confused and take the baby whose name is the same.

Sephardic Jews, on the other hand, do name children for the living and consider it an honor to do so. They often follow a prescribed pattern, using the name of the paternal grandfather for the first boy, the paternal grandmother for the first girl, and so on down the line through the uncles, aunts, etc.[1] Thus, there may be a "Junior" among the Sephardim, but not among the Ashkenazim.

And so, when our first child—a girl—was born, we named her Shayna (Yiddish for "beautiful"), using the first initial of my grandfather's name, Shmuel (Samuel). When our first son followed two years later, we named him Samuel. Using the name of a deceased loved one gives a sense of eternality—his memory is prolonged through the life of the new little one. My father has told me more than once of the pleasure it gives him to know that his father's name lives on.

Later, when we pondered names for our other children, we considered Nathaniel. On mentioning this to my mother, however, we knew we had to look further, as she said through clenched teeth, "You wouldn't dare!" You see, my father's name is Nathan, and that was just too close—it would be "bad luck." My parents feel there is a lot in a name.

A cursory reading of the Jewish Scriptures gives an idea of how important names are to God. He Himself is identified with many names, each one communicating a particular attribute. From the start we see how specific He was in naming His creation, as He called the first man Adam. One of the first things recorded after creation itself is the task given to Adam to name all the animals in the garden. God feels there is a lot in a name.

The first time I read the New Testament, I started in the book of Matthew and was greeted with a barrage of names of people who begot other people. *Why*, I wondered, *would anyone—let alone God—open a book with such a boring beginning?* Little did I realize that the genealogy in Matthew was written with Jewish people in mind. The Messiah had to meet a certain required pedigree, and the only way to verify His identity was to check His claims against the genealogical list in the Temple. Genealogical lists are given in Old Testament books as well—Ezra, Nehemiah, and Chronicles. Once again, there is a lot in a name.

Names can tell a story. Isaac means "laughter" because both Abraham and Sarah laughed when they were told they would become parents in their advanced age. A year later, *Laughter* was born; and from then on, every time they called him by name they were reminded of the miracle God had performed in their lives.

I must say that that passage in Genesis came alive for me when, in January 1984, I took my wife, Alice, to have an ultrasound. "You are going to have twins!" the radiologist told us. Alice cried and I laughed. We didn't name either one Isaac. We chose instead Joanna and Jonathan, both of which mean "gift of God." We know the significance of a name.

Many names in the Bible commemorate events or tell something of the bearers' character. Samuel, the baby for whom Hannah prayed so fervently, means "asked of God." Nabal, the foolish husband of Abigail, means "fool." David, known as the friend of God, means "beloved." One name that is significant to both Jews and Christians is Joshua, or Jesus. They are actually the same name, which translated means "Jehovah is salvation."

There is a long-standing tradition, going back at least two thousand years, of giving two names to children of the Diaspora (dispersion)—those who live and are assimilated into the Gentile world. For instance, my name is Steven. In my neighborhood or in school, I was called Steven. At synagogue, in Hebrew school, or in Sunday school, I was called Yisroel, my Hebrew name. Some Christian commentators think the apostle Paul's name was changed from Saul when he was charged with the responsibility of bringing the gospel to the Gentiles. Actually, being a Roman citizen, I believe he always had the name Paul, although His Jewish name remained Saul. There was a radical change in his focus in life, but his names probably were always the same.

You, dear reader, have a name given to you at birth. Perhaps it is a name you are proud to live up to; perhaps not. Maybe you are known by a nickname that better fits your personality or character. Many names have wonderful meanings that can be a real inspiration in the way we conduct ourselves or the things we strive for in life.

If you are a follower of Jesus the Messiah, you bear His name—Christian. Regardless of your birth name, this alone should be your motivation to be an example of a believer and to live a life pleasing to God.

So, What Exactly Is That?

MEETING NEW PEOPLE IS A REGULAR part of my job. Usually it takes just a short time before I find myself asking the inevitable question, "What do you do?" Sometimes (not often, I hope), the answer leaves me with a rather glazed look. Oh, I hear it all right. But my clueless stare into space is a dead giveaway; I don't have the faintest idea what that particular occupation really is. Then I ask sheepishly, "So, what exactly is that?"

For many people outside the Jewish experience, such words as *kohayn, chazzan, rabbi, rebbe, rav, tzaddik, shammas,* and *gabbai* can produce a similar stare into space. Maybe some of you are familiar with the terms; but you still wonder, "What exactly is that?" Here are the answers to your question.

What Is a Kohayn?

A *kohayn* was a priest in the days of the Jewish Temple in Jerusalem. To understand the term requires a trip into the genealogy of Israel. Jacob, whose name later became Israel, had twelve sons. From them emerged the twelve tribes of Israel. The Levites are descendants of Jacob's son Levi. The Bible describes them as servants around the Holy Temple. Aaron and Moses were Levites. God chose Aaron to perform special duties as the nation of Israel's first high priest. His descendants alone are called *kohanim* (plural of *kohayn*).

When the second Temple was destroyed in A.D. 70, the sacrificial system ended. The genealogical records, which had been kept in the Temple, also were destroyed, making it impossible today to prove any Jewish person's tribal origin. So the title of *kohayn* has been passed down orally from one generation to another. A father assumes he is a *kohayn* because his father told him so, as did his father before him, so on and so forth.

Recent studies in the new field of population research have made several interesting claims. Scientists say the Y-chromosome passes virtually unchanged from father to son. Rabbi Yaakov Kleiman states, "The rare mutations—which are changes in the non-coding portion of its DNA—can serve as markers. Studies have shown a very high genetic affinity among present day Cohanim, indicating that they do have a common paternal ancestor estimated to have lived some 3000 years ago."[1]

Although this research is still in the early stages, it is conceivable that, in the future, people will attempt to identify *kohanim* with a simple blood test. For those Jewish people awaiting the building of a third Temple, this research would be most welcome. Today, individuals thought to be *kohanim* carry the honor and responsibility of being the first to be summoned to read from the Torah in synagogue worship.

WHAT IS A CHAZZAN?

A *chazzan* is a cantor. "What is a cantor?" you may ask. A cantor is the person who leads Jewish worshipers in prayer by chanting and singing the Jewish liturgy. Any person can provide this ministry. But most cantors have recognizable musical talent and have received special training to function in this highly esteemed position within the congregation. They are men (in Orthodox congregations) or sometimes women (in Conservative and Reform congregations) who feel called to such a work.

Jewish worship involves many prayers that are chanted and sung from old, traditional melodies. Larger congregations employ full-time cantors who also spend a good portion of their time training young people in Hebrew education classes, as well as helping them prepare the singing portion of their bat/bar mitzvahs.

What Is the Rabbinate?

The title used for Jewish leaders has varied over the centuries. One title, *rabban* (our master), was used to refer to three presidents of the ancient Sanhedrin (Gamaliel, Simeon Ben-Gamaliel, and Yohanan Ben-Zakkai).[2] Those who followed the teaching of the popular Yohanan Ben-Zakkai and lived outside Israel were called *rav* (master). *Rabbi,* meaning "my master," was bestowed on a person who received his *semikha* (ordination) inside Israel. The word *semikha* literally means to "lean on."[3]

In Numbers 27:18, Moses, as commanded by God, laid his hands on Joshua to appoint him as the next leader. This practice of laying on of hands has been traced from the time of Moses until A.D. 425 when it ended.[4] Jewish ordination today does not include the laying on of hands.

Whichever title one used in those days (*rabban, rav,* or *rabbi*), it signified a talented, scholarly interpreter and expounder of the Scriptures and the oral Law. Later, during the Middle Ages, the meaning and function of a rabbi changed. Prior to the last one hundred years or so, the rabbi in a Jewish community often held a full-time, secular job. He usually received certain privileges, or perks, such as exemption from taxation or preferential treatment in his business. It has never been required that a rabbi be present for a congregation to worship. What is necessary, however, is a quorum of ten men, called a *minyan.*

Today the term *rabbi* simply means "teacher." Although the title can be bestowed on anyone in the Jewish community possessing knowledge and ability in Judaica, today's rabbis usually have received formal seminary training in such subjects as the Jewish Scriptures, Hebrew, Jewish and secular history, and Talmud.

As the Jewish people assimilated into Western culture, the position of rabbi changed. Today rabbis have moved further away from scholarly pursuits and have become more practically oriented for their congregations. Those rabbis who lean toward academia tend to teach in seminaries.

Rabbis have much the same responsibilities as Protestant ministers or pastors. They visit the sick, conduct marriage ceremonies, help families with funeral arrangements, conduct funeral services, help children in the congregation prepare for their bar and bat mitzvahs, and deliver weekly sermons at the Sabbath services.

As in other religions, Judaism has not been immune to the considerable debate and controversy concerning the role of women in the rabbinate. Orthodox Jews have never permitted women rabbis. Some Conservative and all Reform congregations permit women rabbis, and a number have them.

WHAT IS A REBBE?

The small but visible groups of Jewish people called Hasidim use the title *rebbe* for their leader. (This title should not be confused with the word *reb*, which is Yiddish for "mister.") *Rebbe* is a weightier word, sometimes translated as "grand rabbi."[5] Literally, it means "my rabbi." In a Hasidic community, the *rebbe* is the final authority over every decision in a Hasidic Jew's life.

A number of years ago, many Hasidim began to believe that Rebbe Menachem Mendel Schneerson was the long-awaited Messiah of Israel. Marvelous deeds and even miracles were attributed to him. In Israel and in Hasidic communities here in America, signs with his picture are posted, proclaiming, "Prepare for the coming of Messiah." Rebbe Schneerson died in 1994, but many of his followers believe he will rise from the dead.

What Is a Tzaddik?

Tzaddik means "righteous one." The *rebbe* in a Hasidic community is considered a *tzaddik*. But a *tzaddik* does not have to be a *rebbe*. To receive such a designation, one must evidence a spiritual or mystical power.

What Is a Shammas, or Sexton?

Every local congregation always has someone who truly knows the ropes. That someone is the *shammas*. He makes sure everything runs as it should with regard to the physical synagogue building and the scheduling of services. He is the servant of the congregation.

What Is a Gabbai?

A *gabbai* is a volunteer who is knowledgeable in Torah and has the responsibility of coordinating the readers who ascend the platform (*aliyah*) to read from the Torah during a service. It is his responsibility to help them pronounce the Hebrew words or, if need be, to read them himself.

I'm sure my days of asking, "So, what exactly is that?" are far from over. But perhaps now, if you ever hear any of these words in conversation, you won't have to ask the same question. In fact, you may even be able to provide an explanation.

A DAY FOR REMEMBERING
YOM HASHOAH

SOME OF THE MOST DISTURBING WORDS in all of Scripture are found
in the book of Esther:

> *There is a certain people scattered abroad and dispersed*
> *among the people in all the provinces of thy kingdom,*
> *and their laws are different from all people; neither*
> *keep they the king's laws. Therefore, it is not for the*
> *king's profit to tolerate them* (Est. 3:8).

These are Haman's words to Ahasuerus (Xerxes) of Persia
around 500 B.C. Haman's hatred for the Jewish people was not a
secret, so it was no surprise that he wanted all of them—men,
women, and children—killed. As chief advisor, a position of
great trust, he was able to convince Ahasuerus to sign a decree
calling for the extermination of every Jew:

> *The letters were sent by posts into all the king's*
> *provinces, to destroy, to kill, and to cause to perish, all*
> *Jews, both young and old, little children and women,*
> *in one day, even upon the thirteenth day of the twelfth*
> *month, which is the month Adar, and to take the prop-*
> *erty of them for spoil* (Est. 3:13).

The Jewish people were presented as a liability ("not for the king's profit," v. 8) and an inherent danger ("neither keep they the king's laws," v. 8). According to this twisted logic, it was in the best interest of greater Persia to eradicate them and confiscate their assets. By God's grace and providence, Haman failed to achieve his vile aim. Though God's name is not mentioned even once in the entire book, we know He was there all the time.

Throughout history there have been many "Hamans" who have reared their ugly, anti-Semitic heads. The Jewish people have been targets of suffering and destruction most of their existence. They endured four hundred years of slavery in Egypt and saw their holy Temple destroyed by Assyria, then again by Babylon, each time resulting in their removal from their land by force. Since the time of the Diaspora, when the Jews were scattered from their homeland and dispersed to all corners of the world—without a nation, government, or military—generations of men, women, and children have persecuted, driven out, and murdered the Jewish people. Think of the Crusades, the Spanish Inquisition, and the Russian pogroms.

Almost immediately upon emerging as an internationally recognized entity in May 1948, the 650,000 Jewish residents of that new nation of Israel were promised destruction by their 150 million Arab neighbors. In 1991 the shriek of air raid sirens announced the launches of thirty-nine Iraqi Scud missiles. Israelis were forced to huddle in sealed rooms, wearing gas masks and wondering if any of the warheads would bring deadly chemicals attached to them. Today Jewish people are targets for extermination by suicide bombers belonging to organizations with names like Hamas and Islamic Jihad. These bombers perpetrate such attacks while Israelis are waiting for buses, shopping at malls, and eating in restaurants.

However, one event dwarfs all these, standing alone in its ugliness. It was orchestrated by people who were purely evil, possessing the same vision as Haman and the same lust for power. Yet this event produced an unimaginable death toll. It was birthed by satanic hate, nurtured by fear, and sustained by greed. It is called the Holocaust (Hebrew, *Shoah*, meaning "burning"). It resulted in the annihilation of six million men, women, and children whose only crime was being Jewish. No other event in the twentieth century—or ever in history—put such blight on its citizenry.

In 1945 the truth became known to the world as witnesses tried to describe the horror of the Holocaust. Gen. Dwight D. Eisenhower, supreme commander of the allied forces during World War II, once said, "The same day I saw my first horror camp, I visited every nook and cranny. I felt it my duty to be in a position from then on to testify about these things in case there ever grew up at home the belief or assumption that the stories of Nazi brutality were just propaganda."[1]

Much has happened since Eisenhower spoke those words. Voices have arisen with a call to move on. But as one eyewitness to the liberation stated, "I would not believe it had happened in civilized nations. I pray to God that this cannot happen again."[2]

Actively remembering (Hebrew, *zachor*) is incredibly important for the Jewish people. They remember their redemption from slavery in Egypt at Passover, their deliverance from the Persians at Purim, and their deliverance from Antiochus at Hanukkah. Each of these days celebrates the preservation of the Jewish people. There is great joy in celebrating their deliverance.

Yet there is no joy in remembering the Holocaust. Establishing a day of remembrance for the Holocaust was not something Jewish people wanted; it was something they needed. Almost immediately after the establishment of the nation of Israel in 1948, a debate began between Israelis as to how and when to remember the Holocaust. They considered several dates. One was the tenth of *Tevat* (December–January), a day the Jewish people remember the siege of Jerusalem in 586 B.C., confirmed in 2 Kings 25:1. They rejected this suggestion because it had no connection to the Holocaust.

Many wanted the date of the Warsaw Ghetto uprising, April 19, 1943, to provide a direct link to the events of the Holocaust; but they rejected this date because it is too close to Passover.[3] A stalemate ensued until 1950 when they selected an alternate date of 27 *Nisan*. Falling beyond Passover, it is close to the time of the Warsaw Ghetto uprising. Many Orthodox Jews felt it was wrong to have it anytime in the month of *Nisan* because of Passover, but they reached a compromise by saying that, if it fell on the Sabbath, it would move to the next Sunday, which would be in the next month.

And so it was that the Knesset (Israel's parliament) proclaimed April 12, 1951, *Yom Hashoah U'Mered HaGetaot*, Holocaust and Ghetto Revolt Remembrance Day. It was later changed to *Yom Hashoah Ve Hagevurah* (Devastation and Heroism Day). Today it is simply called *Yom Hashoah*.[4]

Yom Hashoah is not a day to celebrate but to remember. How? What do people do? The answer to those questions depends on the people or organization remembering the day. Jewish community centers, synagogues, and individuals observe this day in varied ways. For instance, ceremonies are held in which six candles are lit, each candle representing one million Jewish deaths. In conjunction with the candle lighting, prayers and/or poems are recited. Sometimes people choose to abstain from food to identify with the many who were starved.

Holocaust museums also host varied programs. These remembrances usually include a reading of the names of those who died. Heartwarming stories are often told of the little things done during that time to keep hope alive or to celebrate Jewish community.

One such story took place in Auschwitz, the infamous death camp. It was December, the time of cold winter and Hanukkah. The Jews there wanted to celebrate this Festival of Lights but had no candles to do so. The Nazis certainly would not provide them with candles, so the people saved small portions of butter until they had enough to make one candle. They gathered around secretly and had the rabbi recite the blessings.

The third blessing stated, "We thank God for bringing us to this day." Several asked the rabbi how he could pray such a prayer. The rabbi wondered as well until he looked at all the faces, emaciated, yet glowing, from the light of the candle. "I . . . had to bless Hashem [God], for allowing me to live to see this assembly of martyrs who sanctify the name of G-d in public, who keep their faith amidst the flames," he answered.[5]

The need to remember in the midst of such horror is an amazing response indeed. That desire to remember might seem difficult for most Americans, at least until September 11, 2001. Since that awful day, people in America are now discussing various ways to remember the thousands of people killed by the terrorist attack in New York City and Washington, D.C.

The need for a day like *Yom Hashoah* becomes clearer in light of events that took place in 2001 in Durban, South Africa. At this meeting, attended by members of the United Nations, the world witnessed anti-Semitism in visual form, the likes of which have not been seen since Germany in the 1930s. Cartoon pamphlets depicting Jews as pigs and monkeys were passed out before the conference. Literature was distributed accusing Israel of being an apartheid regime that commits racist crimes against humanity, including ethnic cleansing. It was vile. The UN High Commissioner Mary Robinson, to her credit, dramatically stood up in one of the meetings to express her outrage. As a Gentile woman she declared, "I am a Jew."[6] So outrageous was this conference, in fact, that the United States and Israel left it under protest.

Remembering the Holocaust is essential.

Foreign Minister Shimon Peres made this announcement before leaving the conference:

> In 53 years since the establishment of Israel we were attacked five times with an attempt to overpower us and bring an end to the State of Israel. We stand alone, outnumbered, outgunned, and we defended our lives. We won all the wars; we won a lot of territories. We

gave back the territories, the water, the oil to Egypt. We gave back the land, the water to Jordan. We have withdrawn unilaterally from Lebanon in accordance with UN resolution 425. We offered the Syrians an exchange of land for peace; we have offered the Palestinians something that no Arab country did before us because the West Bank and the Gaza strip were under Arab control. We offered them an independent state. They rejected it. Instead there was the Intifada, and even today there were four bombs in Jerusalem the capital of Israel.[7]

Remembering the Holocaust is essential.

As Christians, should we have anything to do with a day devoted to remembering the Holocaust? To answer that question, I will ask another question. How could we not? As Christians, we should remember an event that so epitomizes the satanic influence held over so many people and countries, especially when we see it fresh today.

Yom Hashoah reminds us of the suffering at the hands of an evil regime, the Nazis; but it also reminds us of the goal of all anti-Semitism. Instigated by Satan himself, it is his attempt to destroy the apple of God's eye, His people, Israel.

As the Jewish people must remember the Holocaust, we must pray for and remember them before the Lord. We must stand by Israel.

THE CALL OF THE SHOFAR

HAVE YOU EVER BEEN DRIVING ALONG the highway when, seemingly out of nowhere, you hear the shrill sound of sirens? At first you are startled as the high-pitched sound seems to engulf you from almost every direction. Instinctively you try to locate the vehicles producing the loud, echoing sounds. At the same time, you begin to ease your car over to the side of the road, as the law requires. Finally you spot the vehicles responsible for all the ruckus and watch them as they speed to wherever the problem is located.

The sound of the siren may be annoying, but it is a necessary and effective attention-getting device. Today the wails of sirens in our cities seem much too commonplace, but when they sound, most people take them seriously and usually respond in dutiful and appropriate fashion.

Throughout Jewish history, we find a record of a particular sound that prompts a certain action, as the response to a siren. This sound, not especially pleasing to the ear, is recognized by the Jewish people in much the same way as a Scotsman or Irishman responds to bagpipes. The source of this unique sound comes from the oldest wind instrument in the world. It is called a *shofar*.

The shofar is a ram's horn. It is very difficult to blow and is done in a way similar to, but not exactly like, a trumpet. In fact, the word *shofar* is often translated *trumpet* in Scripture. The shofar is most often linked to the account in Genesis 22, in which Isaac was to be offered as a sacrifice. The Angel of the Lord interceded just as Abraham drew his knife to kill Isaac. In Isaac's stead, a ram—caught in a thicket by his horns—was sacrificed. As one rabbi explained, we blow the shofar because "The Holy One, blessed be He, said, 'Sound before me a ram's horn so that I may remember on your behalf the binding of Isaac the son of Abraham and account it to you as if you had bound yourselves before me.'"

The Jewish Scriptures record numerous times on which the shofar sounded. The first time was in Exodus 19:16, when its blast acknowledged the presence of God before His people. Leviticus 25:9–10 records that it was sounded to herald the year of Jubilee, signaling the release of slaves and debt, to "proclaim liberty throughout all the land unto all the inhabitants thereof." You may recognize this verse as engraved on America's famous Liberty Bell. Joshua 6 records the shofar sounding just before the walls of Jericho came tumbling down. Ehud blew the shofar to call the Israelites to battle against the Moabites (Jud. 3:27). The sound of the shofar was heard as the people went to the fortified cities in Jeremiah 4:5. It was blown to warn of danger as enemies tried to stop the rebuilding of the walls of Jerusalem: "In whatever place ye hear the sound of the trumpet, resort ye there unto us. Our God shall fight for us" (Neh. 4:20). When a new king took the throne, the shofar would sound a loud blast (1 Ki. 1:5–39).

Bible prophecy states that the sound of the shofar will be heard when the Messiah comes (Zech. 9:14), as it will when the Jewish people return to their land (Isa. 27:13).

Moving forward in history, the shofar continued to hold great significance for the Jewish people, even as it came to be used for other occasions. During the Middle Ages, it was sounded to announce deaths and to mark the beginning of the Sabbath. The shofar served as a reminder of God's giving of the law at Sinai, the belief being that when Moses received the Ten Commandments the second time, he blew the ram's horn to remind the people not to sin, as they had done when they built the golden calf. At this time, too, began the ritual of sounding the shofar on each day during *Elul*, the Hebrew month preceding Rosh Hashanah.[1] It was to be a daily reminder of God's sovereignty and mankind's need to repent.

The shofar's jubilant sound was heard in 1967 when Israeli paratroopers captured East Jerusalem and properly restored the capital of Israel. It was blown at the Western Wall by the chief rabbi of Israel. Today the shofar is sounded in Israel to inaugurate new presidents and prime ministers, reminiscent of the days when the nation had kings.

One of the sages of Israel listed ten reasons to sound the shofar today:

1. To proclaim the sovereignty of God, because it was used at the coronation of kings.

2. To herald the beginning of the Ten Days of Awe (the time between Rosh Hashanah and Yom Kippur).

3. As a reminder of the giving of the Law and the need for faithfulness.

4. As a reminder of the prophets who loudly sounded their voices to a world that needed to hear.

5. As a reminder of the destruction of the Temple.

6. As a reminder of the *Akedah* ("substitute" for Isaac).

7. To inspire awe.

8. As a summons to the heavenly court on the Day of Judgment.

9. As a call to the Jewish remnant to come home.

10. As a reminder of the resurrection.

Maimonides said, concerning the sounding of the shofar, "Awake, O sleepers, from your sleep, O slumberers, arouse ye from your slumbers and examine your deeds. Return in repentance and remember your creator."

According to the Talmud, rams' horns are the horns of choice, but the horns of almost any other kosher animal can be used, including sheep, goats, antelopes, and gazelles. Only cow and calf horns are forbidden, due to the incident described in Exodus 32, when the children of Israel fashioned a golden calf.

The rabbis say that merely listening to the sound of the shofar is not enough. To derive any real meaning from it, the listener must concentrate on the sound. Some rabbis have gone even further, teaching that redemption itself could be wrought "through the horns of the ram" (Rabbah 29:10, Talmudic commentary on Leviticus). It is also believed that Satan becomes confused when the shofar is sounded. For this reason, it sounds often on Rosh Hashanah, trying to prevent him from charging anyone with sin before the Day of Judgment.

Three sounds are basic to the blowing of the shofar. *Tekiah* is a short blast that ends abruptly. This is described (though not by name) in Numbers 10:5–8, as is the second type, *teruah*, which consists of nine staccato blasts. *Shevarim* is three short blasts. One long, sustained sound is called *tekiah gedolah*, or the *great tekiah*. On Rosh Hashanah, the sounds are called out in a particular order:

> *Tekiah—shevarim—teruah—tekiah—tekiah—
> shevarim—tekiah—tekiah—teruah—tekiah gedolah.*

Unless it is the Sabbath, when the shofar is silent, most congregations will hear one hundred blasts from the shofar on each of the two days of Rosh Hashanah. The reason is given in Psalm 89:15: "Blessed are the people that know the joyful sound." Because hearing the sound of the shofar is a blessing, one can expect to hear one hundred blasts as the Day of Atonement approaches.

It is required that the person who blows the shofar must be of sound religious and pietistic character. He should be familiar with the laws and traditions surrounding his awesome task.

Two blessings are recited over the blowing of the shofar. The first is said as a reminder of the command to hear the sound, and the second is to thank God for being present at the time of the blowing.

The greatest sounding of the shofar is yet to come, "at the last trump; for the trumpet shall sound, and the dead shall be raised incorruptible, and we shall be changed" (1 Cor. 15:52). The shofar will blast as Messiah Jesus calls His saints (the church) to meet Him in the air. For us, as believers, it won't be the shrill warning of the siren, but the call to go and be with our Lord forevermore.

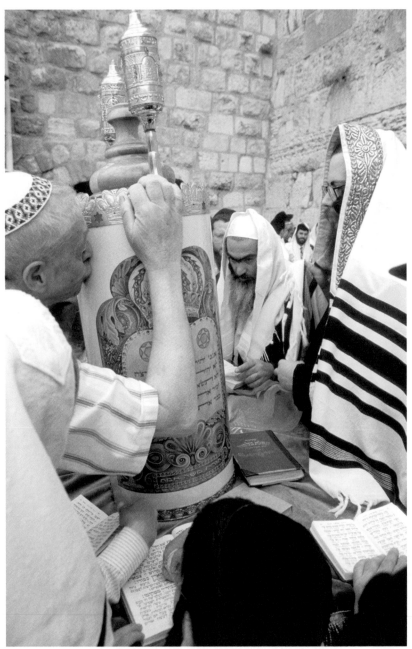

Priestly Blessing Ceremony at the Western Wall in Jerusalem during Passover.

GIVING AND RECEIVING THE BLESSING

DO YOU REMEMBER THE OLD TV PROGRAM *Star Trek*? In that series, the expression "Live long and prosper" became a familiar utterance. It was used by First Officer Spock as a greeting and a farewell to special people visiting the starship *Enterprise*. Spock would raise his right hand, making sure his palm faced the person he was addressing, then position his middle finger away from his ring finger, resting it against his index finger. In turn, his ring finger would be placed against his little finger, forming a V.

Leonard Nimoy, the Jewish actor who played the Vulcan officer in *Star Trek*, said he adapted this unique greeting from the tradition used by the Jewish priests when they invoked the Aaronic blessing. Found in Numbers 6:24–26, it reads "The Lord bless thee, and keep thee; The Lord make his face shine upon thee, and be gracious unto thee; The Lord lift up his countenance upon thee, and give thee peace." Known also as the "priestly blessing," the Aaronic blessing is so called because God said to Moses (v. 23), "Speak unto Aaron and unto his sons, saying, In this way ye shall bless the children of Israel."

WHO RECITES THE BLESSING?

In the days of the Tabernacle and the Temple, the *kohanim*, meaning "priests of Israel," led worship for God's ancient people. These descendants of Aaron were a special group that God set apart to serve Him and to bless the children of Israel (Num. 6:23). In addition, they were responsible for performing the daily rites around the Temple, inspecting animals for disease before sacrifices, and pronouncing people either clean or unclean, thus determining whether they were fit for worship. Priests would ascend a platform (*dukhan*), raise their hands (*nesiat kapavim*) in the manner previously described, and pronounce the blessing. In Yiddish this practice is called *dukhenen*—the delivering of the priestly blessing. The only reason not to follow this command would be if the priest were disqualified through some defilement. Today, some two thousand years after the Temple's destruction, *dukhenen* is still recited by "kohanim."

This giving of the blessing, however, is no longer restricted to the priests or the priestly line. The destruction of the Temple in A.D. 70 brought about the annihilation of all genealogical records. Therefore, no Jewish person today can ascertain his tribal ancestry. Families with the last name *Cohen*, or other derivations of *Kohane*, lay claim to being descendants of priests.

Each Sabbath a parent, preferably the father, will place his hands over the head of each of his children and pronounce the blessing. This practice takes place just before the blessing on the wine.

WHEN IS THE BLESSING RECITED?

Some synagogues include the blessing as part of their everyday prayers. Others prefer to invoke it on the three pilgrim feasts of Passover, Pentecost (Shavuot), and Tabernacles (Sukkot, Dt. 16:16).

One very special time the blessing is used is during the *Pidyon ha ben*—the redeeming of the firstborn. Originally, the children of

Israel were to set apart their firstborn males to the Lord (Num. 8:18). However, because of sin at Sinai, the tribe of Levi was chosen in their stead and separated for service in the sanctuary. Numbers 18:15–16 provides for the formal redemption of the firstborn from the priesthood. Other occasions when this blessing is invoked include weddings and bar and bat mitzvahs.

What Do the Words Mean?

The blessing is actually three blessings written in three specific Hebrew sentences. Although they sound similar, a careful reading reveals a clear order.

"The Lord bless thee" comes first because, regardless of the identity of the person invoking the blessing or the time it is said, the request acknowledges that only God the Creator can provide the blessing. He alone is the provider of all the things needed in life. At the same time, there is the hope that the Creator will guard from evil the person so blessed, thus the statement "and keep thee."

The next Hebrew sentence expresses a desire that God's presence will be with the person being blessed. "The Lord make his face shine upon thee." This second phrase expresses the desire that God would do more than we deserve. Moses was an Israelite. When he was on the mountain at Sinai, the people feared that something had happened to him (Ex. 32:1). Yet what had happened was beyond belief, for this man Moses had spoken with God face to face (Ex. 33:11). That was a special relationship only Moses enjoyed. Thus the second blessing carries the idea of God's presence abiding with the person. There is a desire for God to smile on him. "In biblical idiom the king shows favor to his subjects by giving the audience access to the light of his face. Conversely, the king shows disfavor by hiding his face."[1] This imagery of God causing His face to shine is also seen in passages such as Psalm 80:3, 7 and 19. In addition, the hope is that God will be gracious or kind to the one being blessed.

The third Hebrew sentence in this blessing is, "The Lord lift up his countenance upon thee, and give thee peace." The Hebrew seems to carry the idea of God turning his face toward the one being blessed, literally to face him. If the God of the universe faces us, we will enjoy His favor. The desire, then, is for shalom—peace—not simply the absence of hostility but an expression of divine friendship in keeping with the covenant relationship God promised to His people.

Each of these three blessings is made up of three words and seven words respectively. The second word of each blessing is *Adonai* (Lord), the center, the provider of the blessing.

HOW IS THE BLESSING GIVEN?

The priests extended their arms in front of their chests. They faced their palms toward the crowd with their thumbs touching each other. Each hand set the fingers in such a way to form a V.

When a parent blesses his child, he places his hands upon the child's head as he pronounces the blessing.

DOES THIS RELATE TO THE CHURCH?

For any follower of Christ, the desire to see loved ones blessed and protected by God is genuine. The believer falls heir to this blessing because of Christ's satisfactory payment for sin and for sin's consequence of separation from God. The transaction was made at the cross of Calvary. We are blessed, protected, given peace, and enjoy communion with God that is superior to any that Old Testament priests could bestow.

The best way to impart this blessing to our loved ones is to share the Good News with them and pray that they will receive Messiah as Savior. The fictitious Vulcan greeting cannot compare to the fathomless blessings that will follow for the believer. Instead of living long, they will live forever; and instead of prospering, they will flourish.

ALIYAH FOR THE PEOPLE OF THE BOOK

"THE PEOPLE OF THE BOOK." WHOM do you think of when you hear that phrase, which so clearly distinguishes a specific people? Which people and what book?

The people are the Chosen People, the Israelites of old and their progeny—the Jewish people of today, the descendants of Abraham, Isaac, and Jacob.

The Book, of course, is the Bible. Its author is the God of Abraham, Isaac, and Jacob, the One who chose the Jewish people "to be a special people unto himself, above all people who are upon the face of the earth" (Dt. 7:6). And the book they hold so dear is no ordinary book. It is written on parchment, sewn together, rolled onto wooden rollers called *eytz chayeem* (tree of life), and read regularly in the synagogue. They call these scrolls of the Law *Torahs*. The word *Torah* comes from the verbal root that means "to guide" or "to instruct." Jewish liturgy proclaims Torah a "tree of life to those who hold fast to it."[1]

Most Jewish people today don't consider themselves special, chosen, or even particularly religious. Nor does the vast majority spend much time at home reading the more ordinary copies of this special Book. Yet almost all Jewish people would say the

Torah scrolls themselves are extremely important, even more so than their contents. Some Jewish people even believe that just to gaze or look upon the holy Torah scrolls can produce a blessing. Therefore, it is not surprising that to possess a Torah scroll is considered a great honor.

And to ascend to the *bima* (platform) of a synagogue; take the *yad* (silver pointer) in hand; and, like Ezra of old, read aloud the Word of God is considered an enormous privilege. Today, when Jewish people gather publicly to worship, a specific number of men are honored with the opportunity to make *aliyah*—to go up to the Torah to say the blessings and, perhaps, read from the unrolled scroll. In fact, the word *aliyah* means "ascend" or "go up." To qualify for such an honor, you must be recognized as a legitimate member of the Jewish people. The centrality of these scrolls to Judaism is not taken lightly.

Before the Torah can be read, a minimum of ten men, a *minyon*, must assemble for the event. Deuteronomy 31:10–13 is the first reference to the public reading of God's Word:

> *Thou shalt read this law before all Israel in their hearing. Gather the people together, men, and women, and children, and thy sojourner who is within thy gates, that they may hear, and that they may learn, and fear the LORD your God, and observe to do all the words of this law* (vv. 11–12).

The book of Nehemiah records that the Jewish people—male, female, old, and young—stood for half the day to listen to God's Word (8:1–8).

When the Sephardic Jews (those of Mediterranean descent) gather, they open the scroll and lift it up in full view of the congregation *before* reading the Torah. In Ashkenazi congregations (those of Eastern European descent), the Torah is lifted *after* it is read. Either way, the congregation chants, "This is the law which Moses set before the children of Israel" (Dt. 4:44).

Four events in a person's life virtually mandate that he receive an *aliyah*. The first of these is the birth of a child. Certainly, any birth is a "blessed event." But in a Jewish home, at least part of the rejoicing takes place around the Word of God. If the baby is a girl, she receives her name after her father has made *aliyah* at the synagogue on the Sabbath following her birth. There he publicly speaks his daughter's name for the first time. If the baby is a boy, the father makes *aliyah* after the *brit milah*, or covenant of circumcision, which takes place eight days after the child's birth. That, too, is when the father publicly speaks his son's name aloud for the first time.

The first opportunity for Jewish people to read from a scroll is when they turn thirteen. The event is the *bar mitzvah* (meaning "son of the commandment") for boys and, in some synagogues, the *bat mitzvah* for girls (daughter of the commandment). For many Jewish people, these events become the defining moments of their lives. Almost every Jewish person I have met who has ascended the platform to be recognized as a son or daughter of the commandment vividly remembers reading from the scroll in front of friends and family for the first time.

The third life-cycle event requiring *aliyah* takes place the Sabbath before a wedding. The bridegroom goes up to read from the holy scroll. When he is finished, the congregation pummels him with candy, a practice believed to insure a sweet life. It is a remarkably holy and hilarious time for both the bridegroom and the congregation. Recently a well-known talk show host elaborated on this custom as he anticipated his brother "finally" getting married. "We are going to throw a little harder," he said, "because he kept us waiting thirty-nine years."

The fourth important *aliyah* comes on the Sabbath before observing *yahrzeit*, the anniversary of the death of an immediate family member. A solemn goodbye is marked by reading the Word of the God who gives and takes life.

It is noteworthy that, regardless of whether an event gives great joy or great sadness, the Jewish thing to do is to declare

God's Word by reading it in public. This declaration is so important that, before it takes place, the individual called on to read from the sacred scroll must recite two blessings. The first says,

> *Bless the Lord who is blessed. Blessed is the Lord who is forever blessed. Blessed art Thou, O Lord our God, King of the universe, who has chosen us from among all peoples by giving us Thy Torah. Blessed art Thou, O Lord, giver of the Torah.*

The second blessing states,

> *Blessed art Thou, O Lord our God, King of the universe, who has given us Thy Torah of truth and thereby planted among us life eternal. Blessed art Thou, O Lord, giver of the Torah.*

So holy, so magnificent is the scroll that the reader takes his *talit* (prayer shawl), touches it to the parchment, then brings his hand to his mouth. It is a holy kiss.

For some Jewish people, reading from the Torah and making *aliyah* is the dramatic reenactment of the theophany at Sinai.[2]

It is believed that the reader is in the abode of the Almighty. The person called to read represents the people to whom the Torah was given; and the *segan*, the congregational leader who apportions the *aliyyot* (plural of *aliyah*) and stands beside the reader, has the role of Moses.

Although the privilege of *aliyah* is significant in these four life-cycle events, individuals can receive *aliyyot* at other times. On *Shabbat* (Sabbath), one of the most important days on the Jewish calendar, up to seven *aliyyot* are given. These seven slots must be filled by individuals from prescribed groups of people. One of the seven has to be a *kohayn*, a descendant of Aaron. He is regarded as a possible high priest. Another spot must be taken by a *Levite*, a person from the priestly tribe. The other five positions are filled by men from the congregation, "Israelites," sometimes called in Hebrew the *am ha'aretz* (the people of the land). These persons can be from any tribe except Levi. Of course, no one today knows for certain what tribe he is from. Jewish people must take an educated guess.

So it is that a certain people, the people of the Book, ascend to read and listen to the Word of the Lord. This tradition has been practiced by Jews for thousands of years and is the method God has used to teach and instruct His people.

Luke 4 records an *aliyah* that was unprecedented and unrepeatable. The portion of Scripture to be read that day was Isaiah 61:1–2. The person chosen to read it was Jesus, a legitimate Israelite who knew with absolute certainty that He was from the tribe of Judah. Luke 4:16–19 records the event:

> *He came to Nazareth, where he had been brought up; and, as his custom was, he went into the synagogue on the sabbath day, and stood up to read. And there was delivered unto him the book of the prophet, Isaiah. And when he had opened the book, he found the place where it was written, The Spirit of the Lord is upon me, because he hath anointed me to preach the gospel to the poor; he hath sent me to heal the brokenhearted, to preach deliverance to the captives, and recovering of sight to the blind, to set at liberty them that are bruised, To preach the acceptable year of the Lord.*

On completing those words, Jesus did something dramatic, something so unusual it stunned the congregation. He stopped, closed the Book, sat down, and said, "This day is this scripture fulfilled in your ears" (Lk. 4:21). Jesus used his *aliyah* to testify of His identity as the Messiah of Israel. Unfortunately, His offer was rejected. And it would be rejected many more times by many others who did not believe the Word. His *aliyah* was unique; but its results were not. People still decline to consider God's Word.

Time after time in our collective history and in our individual lives, His Word has gone unheeded, even rejected. Although it is a great honor and privilege to make *aliyah* and read from the

Torah, it is but a fleeting moment of glory with no lasting value unless the Words of God inscribed there grip the soul of the reader. Will the people of the Book obey the Book? The answer to that question is of eternal significance.

The prophet Micah (4:1–2) and his contemporary, Isaiah (Isa. 2:2–4), told of a future time when all will accept God's Word. Both men recorded this prophecy:

> *In the last days it shall come to pass, that the mountain of the house of the LORD shall be established in the top of the mountains, and it shall be exalted above the hills, and people shall flow unto it. And many nations shall come, and say, Come, and let us go up to the mountain of the LORD, and to the house of the God of Jacob; and he will teach us of his ways, and we will walk in his paths; for the law shall go forth from Zion, and the word of the LORD from Jerusalem* (Mic. 4:1–2).

That *aliyah* will be special indeed.

BLESSINGS ON YOUR HEAD

AT THE BEGINNING OF THE MOVIE *Fiddler on the Roof,* Jewish people in the little Russian village of Anatevka ask their rabbi if there is a special blessing for the czar. The czar ruled the country and was no friend to the Jewish people. The rabbi ponders a moment, then breaks into a huge grin as he replies, "A blessing for the czar? May the Lord bless and keep the czar [short pause] far away from us!"

As most Jewish people know, Judaism has a *barukha* (blessing or benediction) for just about everything. For devout Jews, worship of the one true God is woven into every aspect of their lives. He is considered the Creator and Sustainer of all life and the One who holds the universe in the palm of His hand. It is said that the word *blessing* "is not a verb describing what we do to God; it is an adjective describing God as the source of all blessing."[1]

A blessing is viewed as a reminder of the incredible, awesome power of the Lord and as a declaration of the desire for Him to use that power for good. *Barukhas,* or *barukhot* (Hebrew plural), are good. Jewish tradition states that a person should recite one hundred *barukhot* each day. Thus there is no shortage of them in and out of the Jewish Scriptures.

The Hebrew word *barukha* comes from the verb *brkh*, which means "to fall on one's knees."[2] It is a built-in reminder to the Jewish people of man's position in relationship to God.

Jewish Scripture overflows with *barukhas*. Genesis 24:27 records the *barukha* of Abraham's servant when he spotted Rebekah, the future bride for Isaac, Abraham's son: "Blessed be the LORD God of my master, Abraham, who hath not left destitute my master of his mercy and his truth." Exodus 18:10 records the *barukha* of Jethro, Moses' father-in-law, when he said, "Blessed be the LORD, who hath delivered you out of the hand of the Egyptians." Ruth 4:14 records the women's *barukha* over Naomi when they realized there was a near kinsman who could marry her widowed daughter-in-law, Ruth: "Blessed be the LORD, who hath not left thee this day without a kinsman, that his name may be famous in Israel." These are but a few of the *barukhas* in the Bible.

A familiar *barukha* is often heard when someone sneezes. Most Jewish people nearby will immediately offer up a "God bless you" or "*Gezundheit,*" ("to your health"). Jewish legend associates the sneeze with life and death. Genesis 2:7 says God blew into Adam's nostrils "the breath [soul] of life." Since the nostrils are the portals through which life enters and departs, this blessing expresses the desire that God continue to sustain the sneezer.

Barukhas are key in the prayer lives of Jewish people. Although they can be recited when you're alone, most blessings are recited in a gathering of at least ten people (a *minyan*).

BLESSINGS IN THE MORNING

Jewish observance requires that each day start with the recitation of blessings. The day begins with the blessing for washing the hands and continues with the blessings for God's creation and sustenance and for the privilege of beginning a new day. During the day there are blessings for the study of Torah. Here are some examples:

Barukh Hu

The leader of the congregation begins the prayer by saying, *"Barkhu et Adonai ha-mevorah"* ("Bless the Lord who is blessed"). The congregants respond by bending their knees and saying, "Blessed is the Lord who is blessed for eternity."

Barukh She-amar

The daily morning service includes the recitation of the *Barukh She-amar* ("Blessed be He who spoke"). It begins a prayer, wrote scholar Philip Birnbaum, "composed of eighty-seven words, a number suggesting the numerical value of [the Hebrew word for] refined gold."[3]

Barukh Shem Kevod

This phrase, *Blessed be His glorious majesty forever and ever*, accompanies the opening verse of the *Shema* (Dt. 6:4–9). The Talmud, an extrabiblical book, claims that Jacob spoke these words right before his death when he asked his sons about their spiritual condition. They reportedly quoted the *Shema*, and Jacob recited the benediction immediately afterward.[4]

BLESSINGS FOR FOOD

One of God's wonderful blessings is food. Judaism encourages prayer both before and after eating. Deuteronomy 8:10 states, "When thou hast eaten and art full, then thou shalt bless the LORD thy God for the good land which he hath given thee." Thus all blessings recited for food begin with the words, *Barukh atta Adonai Eloheinu melekh ha-olam* ("Blessed art Thou, O Lord our God, King of the Universe").

The blessings said prior to eating begin the same way but have different endings, depending on the food to be eaten. For wheat products, the prayer ends with *hamotzi lechem mein ha-aretz*, which blesses God for the wheat from the ground. For wine, the ending is *borai pre hagofen*, which blesses God for the fruit of the vine. For vegetables from the ground, the prayer is *borai pre ha-a-da-ma*, which blesses God for the food from the earth.

Perhaps unique to Judaism is the requirement for prayer *after* one eats. As a boy, I attended an Orthodox summer camp. One of my frustrations was how long it took for lunch. After saying the blessings before eating, then eating and praying after eating, it seemed as though the afternoon was over. Although that wasn't really the case, the liturgy did require at least twenty minutes. This liturgy is known among Ashkenazi (European) Jews as *benshn*. It is a Yiddish word derived (by way of German) from the Latin word *benedicere*, meaning "bless, pronounce a benediction."[5] It is known as the *Birkat ha-Mazon* (grace after meals).

There are four parts to this liturgy. *Birkat ha-Zan* praises God for providing food for the world. *Birkat ha-Aretz* expresses Israel's gratitude for the good land God has given the Jewish people, for bringing them out of the land of Egypt, and for giving them the Torah. *Boneh Yerushalayim* asks God to have mercy on Israel and to restore the Temple, the Kingdom of God, and the Messiah's work. And finally, *Ha-tov-ve-ha-metiv* thanks God for His goodness and works and also includes a number of requests.[6]

According to tradition, three of the blessings originated from actual events recorded in the Bible. They involve Moses and the manna, Joshua and the land, and Kings David and Solomon and the kingdom. The fourth blessing came from the rabbis.

The Diaspora (scattering of the Jewish people) resulted in different *barukhas* developing in different areas of the world. According to the Talmud, this *"barukha* diversity" is limited in only two ways: Each prayer "must have the name of God, and . . . must also contain the attribute of God's kingship."[7]

Noted rabbi Adin Steinsaltz defined prayer as a "direct and unequivocal act of relating to God. . . . Prayer is essentially one thing: an explicit addressing by the human 'I' to the divine 'Thou.'" It is, he said, "the salient expression of religious emotion in man and of his relationship with his Creator."[8] The rabbi eloquently explained the essence of prayer.

HEAD COVERINGS

Understanding the place God is to hold in the prayer lives of Jewish people explains the use of blessings. It also sheds light on an important custom (some Jewish people call it a command) of covering the head. "Jewish tradition regards bare headedness as a form of nakedness, and nudity as one of pagan indecencies and an infraction of propriety in worship," explained Birnbaum.[9] This tradition is based on two Hebrew words used in Deuteronomy that refer to anything indecent. Not a single place in the Old Testament contains a command for men to wear head coverings. It is true that the high priest wore a miter, and the priests covered their heads (Ex. 28:4); but that is all.

There are different names for the covering. Most Jewish people call it a *yarmulke* (pronounced *yah*-ma-kah). This is a Yiddish word, derived from the Aramaic phrase *yira malka*, which means "fear of the King."[10] The Hebrew term is *kippah*.

Many reasons are given why Jewish men should cover their heads. While attending Hebrew school, I was told that Jewish men needed to cover their heads to remind them not to be such big shots—that someone is higher and mightier than they. Indeed, the covering is to be a reminder of the awesome power and might of the God of Abraham, Isaac, and Jacob.

Today Hasidic and Orthodox Jewish men cover their heads at all times because the Talmud teaches that men should not walk four steps without their heads covered (Shabbath 118b.) They believe that once a male reaches the age of three, he should cover his head. In many synagogues, a box of *kippot* (plural) sits at the sanctuary entrance; any man who does not have his own *kippah* can borrow one from there since a *kippah* is required for all men who enter.

Conservative Jewish men wear head coverings only when they worship, whether at home or at synagogue. For other activities, covering the head is not required. Reform Jews are not obligated to cover their heads at all; and, as a result, most do not.

It is not necessary for Jewish women to cover their heads. Yet, because the Torah associates shame and punishment with uncovering a woman's head (Num. 5:18), Hasidic and some Orthodox women choose to cover their heads with scarves or hats. Others will cover their heads only when they light the Sabbath or holiday candles.

As we look at the Jewish liturgy, we see two important aspects regarding blessings: a great devotion to God and the ongoing expression of that devotion. As with any good thing, however, the practice itself can sometimes become more important than the reason for it. That is why, as Christians, we ought to identify strongly with our Jewish friends' pursuit to worship while at the same time making sure the blessings we offer truly come from our hearts.

JUDAISM VS. JEWISHNESS

HE COULD HAVE BEEN A POSTER BOY for a Jewish magazine. Reared in an observant home, he had celebrated his bar mitzvah at age thirteen. He graduated from Hebrew school at the age of eighteen, and it was clear he had a firm grasp of Jewish history and culture as well as an astute understanding of his Jewish heritage. He would go on to teach Sunday school for several years at a highly respected Jewish school in a prominent conservative synagogue. These impeccable credentials, however, were obviously inadequate to alter the direction his life would take. For when I met him, he was no longer teaching, no longer observant, and no longer possessing even a strand of Jewish attachment.

An all-too-common truth is that many Jewish people have turned away from traditional Jewish practice. What might seem truly baffling, however, was this man's reaction to the gospel message presented to him by a Jewish person. Given his non-Jewish lifestyle, he astounded even himself when he said, "I know I have no right to say this because of the way I live my life, but I am deeply offended by your conversion." While personally distancing himself from other Jewish people and the practice of Judaism, he was, nevertheless, Jewish enough to be offended. Was this non-practicing Jewish man still Jewish?

In conversation, a Jewish woman wanted to make one point very clear. Her friend's daughter, she averred, "is no longer Jewish." These poignant words were prompted by a sincere conviction that the girl's personal faith in Jesus as Savior had stripped away her Jewish origin. Was the woman's assessment correct? Had her friend's daughter ceased being Jewish?

What *does* make a person Jewish? This question was asked of another Jewish woman whose daughter was about to marry a man who taught transcendental meditation. The prospective bridegroom graduated from Maharishi University in Iowa, and although born into a Jewish home, he had no allegiance to his Jewish upbringing or to God Himself. The woman's answer? A person remains Jewish *as long as he doesn't believe in Jesus!*

Many Gentiles, particularly believers in the Messiah, are fascinated by Jewish culture and tradition. Some actually adopt various Jewish practices. These include keeping the dietary laws, donning phylacteries, and worshiping on the Sabbath. Are these Gentiles now Jewish? Or are they simply Gentiles engaging in Judaism? Is there a difference between *Jewishness* and *Judaism*?

The term *Judaism* is an elusive one to understand. When Reconstructionist Rabbi Carol Harris-Shapiro was asked, "What is Judaism?" she responded truthfully: "I don't think we are tremendously clear on that."[1]

A cursory look into Jewish periodicals affirms the rabbi's opinion. While numerous articles convey information on biblical history, feast celebrations, and life-cycle events, few provide a specific definition of Judaism itself. The late rabbi and philosopher Milton Steinberg attempted a definition in his book *Basic Judaism.* "Judaism," he said, "denotes a full civilization; the total actualities, past and present, of the historic group of human beings known as the Jewish people."[2] His definition continues, "Just as properly, Judaism may stand for something more limited: the spiritual aspect of that civilization; in sum, for the Jewish religion." Thus Steinberg's estimation is that Judaism embraces both people and religion.

Asher Zvi Ginzburg, known by his famous pen name Ahad Ha-Am (meaning "one of the people"), was a noted author of the late 1800s. He defined *Judaism* "to mean the entire spiritual and intellectual life of the Jewish people of which the Jewish religion was but one expression." He contended that "it was impossible for one to be a Jew in the religious sense without acknowledging nationality, yet it was possible to be a Jew in the national sense without accepting many things in which religion requires belief."[3] For Ginzburg, practice was not nearly as important as nationality.

Thus Gentiles who incorporate Jewish practices into their lives cannot become Jews by virtue of these practices. It takes more than religious practice to be a Jew. Conversely, the former Jewish Sunday school teacher who abandoned Jewish practice and the bridegroom who graduated from a school of Eastern thought do not cease being Jews. They are simply Jews not practicing Judaism. On these points, most members of the Jewish community would agree.

Possessing a messianic hope has long been regarded as foundational to the Jewish identity. Unfortunately, following false messiahs has been part of Jewish history as well. Today thousands of Hasidic Jews strongly believe that deceased Rabbi Menachem Schneerson was a messiah. These are Jewish people who believe they have found their Jewish Messiah. Would anyone say they are no longer Jewish? But what of the Jewish girl described by her mother's friend as "no longer Jewish" because she believes that Jesus, a direct descendant of King David, is the Messiah? This young lady's decision to cease practicing rabbinic Judaism makes her no less Jewish than others who have done likewise.

This logic has not escaped Rabbi Carol Harris-Shapiro. In a July 1999 issue of the *Jewish Exponent*, Brian Mono reported that Rabbi Harris-Shapiro has written a book examining

Jewish people who believe in Jesus as Messiah. Her *Jewishness*, however, has led her to this conclusion: "Maybe it's time to revisit belief as a necessary component of Judaic identity."

Thus it appears that *Jewishness* relates to a person's essence, while *Judaism* relates to his practice. *Jewishness* defines a person's identity, his roots, his heritage as a physical descendant of Jacob. It is a term that explains why a Jewish man can forsake Judaism to seek peace through Eastern thought but is still considered Jewish by his mother-in-law. Ginsberg's analysis, written more than one hundred years ago, is amazingly accurate today. Today Jewish people are practicing atheists, Buddhists, and New Agers; but in essence, they are still Jews. It is their birthright, whether they like it or not. There is just one solitary element— the unpardonable Jewish sin, if you will—that alters that status in the minds of many Jewish people. That element is identifying Jesus Christ as your personal Savior. He and He alone seems to be the line of demarcation. A recent article by R. Albert Mohler Jr., in *World* magazine speaks to this issue:

> The majority of American Jews are now thoroughly secularized, with only a minority confessing belief in a personal God. Major Jewish leaders—Mr. [Alan] Dershowitz included—argue that Jews do not need to believe in God, only in Judaism. The major Jewish groups have closed ranks on the question of Jewish converts to Christianity. A good Jew may be an atheist, but no Jew can believe that Jesus is the Messiah and remain a Jew [emphasis added].[4]

Why do Jewish people feel this way? Many complex issues are involved. The name of Jesus has been invoked for centuries as a reason to kill, rape, and murder Jews. It also has become an integral part of the fabric of Gentile world culture—a culture that has been anything but kind to the Jewish people. Those who have spiritual eyes know that we are in a spiritual battle. Satan hates whom God loves, and God loves the Jewish people.

A chief ingredient to Jewishness is a desire to preserve tradition—to survive. Perhaps this explains why Jewish people who have received Christ seldom forsake their identity as Jews. Certain things do bind the children of Israel together regardless of belief. For some, it is the desire to preserve tradition. For others, it is the knowledge of common heritage as descendants of Abraham, Isaac, and Jacob. A bloodline cannot be denied regardless of outward circumstances or inward beliefs. Though the sentiments behind it may differ, the essence of the saying remains true: "I was born a Jew, and I'll die a Jew."

CHOSEN? FOR WHAT?

WERE YOU EVER THE FIRST ONE ONTO the baseball diamond but the last to be chosen for a team? Or worse, maybe you were never chosen at all? Maybe, though, you were the best player on the field and were always chosen first. For some of us, it was routine for a teacher to choose us to run an errand or perform a special service. Then again, others among us might identify better with the person who volunteered for everything, yet never was selected to do anything. What a wonderful feeling it is to be chosen—to realize you made the team or were selected for something special. Conversely, the pain and humiliation that sometimes come to those who are not chosen can be immense.

Hopefully, this illustration helps explain why the biblical concept of a chosen people evokes such varied responses. Reactions run the gamut from vehement denial and displeasure to excitement and euphoria. And between these extremes, you can always find the people who ask, uninterestedly, "What difference does it make anyway?" This spectrum of reactions comes from Jewish people, Gentiles, and Christians.

Many years ago in Hebrew school, I learned a fanciful Talmudic story that tried to explain how the Jewish people came to be "chosen." God supposedly went to all the nations of the earth, individually, to offer them the opportunity to embrace Torah (Jewish law). Each nation refused to accept the offer because of a difference or disagreement with some aspect of it. But when God came to little Israel with His offer, the response was swift and immediate. It was received with great joy.

The textbook we used during those days was titled *A Treasure Hunt in Judaism*, published by the Hebrew Publishing Company. It explained the concept of Israel as God's Chosen People this way:

> *Think of the world as a large classroom, with God as the teacher. He calls a small pupil, named Israel, to the front of the classroom and says, "Here are ten rules I want the class to observe. Will you please write them on the blackboard so that everybody may see and copy them." And while the class copies from the blackboard, the Teacher sits in a back seat and watches the progress of His pupils. And when I think of this, I get the feeling that perhaps we should be called the Chosen Pupil, who is trying his best to help his Teacher.*[1]

Both explanations helped me to understand clearly that it was God who took the initiative. He chose us. It was up to us to understand the great privilege we had and the responsibility that came with it in order to please Him. Noted author Abraham Hershel affirmed this truth when he said, "There is no concept of a chosen God but there is the idea of a chosen people."[2]

Some Jewish people disagree. Rabbi Mordecai Kaplan (1881–1983) was one. Kaplan founded the Reconstructionist movement within Judaism. He urged his fellow Jews to erase the concept of chosenness, reasoning that being a special people set the tone for a racist ideology and denoted arrogance. In addition, he believed such thinking was divisive, causing distrust and difficulties between people groups.

Many Jewish people agree with Rabbi Kaplan. They either have seen or experienced terrible persecution and know that for hundreds, even thousands, of years, the Jewish people have felt the sting of anti-Semitism. That is why so many Jews invariably ask, "If this is what being 'chosen' means, why couldn't God have chosen somebody else?"

Other Jewish people see the idea of chosenness from an entirely different perspective. A first-century rabbi stated bluntly that God did not choose Israel but, rather, Israel chose God.[3]

Why would Jewish people believe they are the Chosen People? In his well-known book *This is My God*, Pulitzer Prize-winning author Herman Wouk, an Orthodox Jew, gives the clearest and most accurate explanation: "It is the Holy Bible that so describes the Jews. The quotations run into the thousands, the theme rules Scripture."[4] One such verse is Deuteronomy 14:2:

> For thou art an holy people unto the LORD thy God, and the LORD hath chosen thee to be a peculiar people unto himself, above all the nations that are upon the earth.

Martin Buber, a noted Jewish philosopher and theologian, believed that the Hebrew term *am segula*, translated "peculiar people" (Dt. 14:2; 26:18) and "peculiar treasure" (Ex. 19:5), was derived from the Akkadian word meaning "cattle" or "property." He explained that, just as cattle was man's treasured or chosen property in nomadic times, so Israel was considered God's treasured possession.[5]

Rabbi Samson Raphael Hirsch commented on the verse in Deuteronomy this way:

> God's choice of Israel does not imply Israel's exclusive possession of divine love and favor. On the contrary, it means that God has exclusive claim to Israel's service. The most cherished ideal of Israel is that of universal brotherhood. Israel's character as the chosen people does not involve the inferiority of other nations. It was

*the noble obligation of the God-appointed worker for
the entire human race.*[6]

When the Jewish people think about "chosenness," they
emphasize the spiritual aspect:

*Being God's chosen people carried with it greater spir-
itual responsibilities and implied more demanding
standards and the necessity to develop a spiritual vigor
worthy of those whom God had selected to preserve and
transmit his revelation to all the world.*[7]

Thus the idea that Jews believe they are superior to other people is absolutely false. They realize God could indeed have chosen someone else, but He did not. Thus they are obliged to carry
out His will and follow His marching orders.

So why did God choose the Jewish people? Again the text of
Torah, the Jewish Scriptures, provides the answer:

*The LORD did not set his love upon you, nor choose
you, because ye were more in number than any people;
for ye were the fewest of all people. But because the
LORD loved you, and because he would keep the oath
which he had sworn unto your fathers* (Dt. 7:7–8).

God chose Israel based not on her inherent strength but,
rather, on her distinct weakness.

According to Jewish thinking, God chose the Jewish people to
be the source of light in the world. They were to study the rule
of law given to them and obey it—to take the 613 *mitzvot* (365
"thou shalts," 248 "thou shalt nots") and incorporate them into
their daily lives.

Does this kind of thinking affect the way Jewish people view
non-Jews? Is there a Jewish expectation for the way Gentiles are
to live before God? Religiously observant Jewish people often
believe God has placed a minimal biblical standard on all men.
"They [Jews] are obligated to observe the whole Torah, while
every non-Jew is a 'son of the covenant of Noah' and he who
accepts its obligations, is a *gertoshave* (resident stranger)."[8]

Maimonides, a 12th-century rabbi who is considered one of the greatest Jewish thinkers of all time, declared Gentiles as *hassid*, or righteous, if they follow these seven laws:

1. Behave equitably in all relationships and establish courts of justice.

2. Refrain from blaspheming God's name.

3. Refrain from practicing idolatry.

4. Avoid immoral practices, specifically incest.

5. Avoid shedding the blood of one's fellow man.

6. Refrain from robbing one's fellow man.

7. Refrain from eating a limb torn from a live animal.

Orthodox Jewish people used to cite these seven rules as their reasons not to "evangelize" or seek converts to Judaism. They felt it is better for someone to be a righteous Gentile than an unobservant Jew. It is no wonder that a Yiddish proverb states, in utter simplicity, "It is hard to be a Jew."[9]

Noted rabbi and author Joseph Telushkin wrote,

> *Because of the Jews' small numbers, any success they would have in making God known to the world would presumably reflect upon the power of the idea of God. Had the Jews been a large nation with an outstanding army, their successes in making God known would have been attributed to their might and not to the truth of their ideas.*[10]

Historically, evangelical Christians have heartily embraced the biblical teaching that God chose the Jewish people. For them, such issues are settled in God's Word. If God said it, they believe it, and that's all there is to it. The fact that God chose a people to be His own neither intimidates nor infuriates them. To the contrary, many biblical Christians recognize that God not only chose the Jewish people and calls them "the apple of his eye" (Zech. 2:8) but that He has a plan and purpose for them, just as He has a special plan and purpose for His church.

David's attitude before he became king reflects how so many Bible-believing Christians feel toward the Jewish people. David was doing his best to keep one step ahead of being murdered by King Saul. He had numerous opportunities to kill the king. But he refused to do so. Why? He gave the reason to his nephew, Abishai, Joab's brother, in 1 Samuel 26:9: "Destroy him not; for who can stretch forth his hand against the LORD's anointed, and be guiltless?"

David recognized Jehovah as the Sovereign of the universe. God was in charge, and He could choose any king He wanted. David was more fearful of Jehovah than of any Israelite king. He was not going to interfere with God's choice.

Christians should feel the same way about Israel. We know that the same God who chose Israel also chose individual Jews and Gentiles to become part of the body of Christ through faith. Like Israel, there is nothing inherent in any of us that would merit our being chosen and receiving the forgiveness of sin that comes with salvation. It is strictly the gracious and merciful act of an infinite and loving God who is "not willing that any should perish, but that all should come to repentance" (2 Pet. 3:9).

Ultimately, the most important question, perhaps, is not, "Why did God choose the Jewish people?" but, "How can I become chosen?" The answer to that is easy:

> *If thou shalt confess with thy mouth the Lord Jesus, and shalt believe in thine heart that God hath raised him from the dead, thou shalt be saved. For with the heart man believeth unto righteousness; and with the mouth confession is made unto salvation* (Rom. 10:9–10).

When You're Dead, You're Dead

A NUMBER OF YEARS AGO, I ATTENDED the funeral of a dear Jewish friend named Max. I had met him through mutual friends shortly after his right side had become crippled by a stroke. During those last physically challenging years, Max and I got to know each other quite well. Although his death was not unexpected, it was, for many, a very emotional experience. He had left an impact on countless friends and business associates, and a great many came to pay their final respects.

Max was a by-product of his era. He had risen from the rampant anti-Semitism of Eastern Europe and the poverty of an immigrant to become a highly successful and greatly loved businessman. He treated everyone well, customers and employees alike.

At his funeral, many paid him tribute. As the service drew to a close, the rabbi shared some personal information about Max's life. Then he said something I will never forget: "I do not know where Max is right now; but if there is a heaven, I know he is there, happy and rested." The rabbi—a spiritual teacher of his people—had just confessed that he was ignorant concerning Max's future; and most of the congregation seemed comfortable with that. As we left the service, I heard people comment on the "beautiful sermon" the rabbi had given.

Unfortunately, their reactions did not surprise me. Many Gentiles, Christians, and Muslims spend a good deal of time teaching about the afterlife. Judaism, however, does not. A common and popular idea held by many Jewish people is "deed rather than creed." Consequently, many Jewish people resent hearing about death and dying, preferring, rather, to discuss life and living. One rabbi put it this way: "We invest more of our belief in this world (*olam ha-zeh*) and rely less on a world to come (*olam ha-ba*)."

Many Jewish people strongly believe there is no life at all after death. "When you're dead, you're dead," they say. One rabbi has said, "Even as a rabbi I have never departed from my early feeling, when I die the whole world of my existence would die with me."[1] In a published sermon titled "A Jewish View of Immortality," Rabbi Bernard Rascus wrote,

> *What is this immortality in which I believe? I believe that a person lives on in his or her family. . . . I believe there is a form of immortality in the institutions we build and the causes we espouse. . . . I believe in the immortality of friendship and helpfulness. . . . I believe in the immortality of existence. . . . I find immortality in my people.*[2]

Another great sage who lived in Jerusalem in the second century stated, "A man will live on through his children."[3] Others believe their immortality comes through their deeds, as this Talmudic story explains:

> *A hungry fox was eyeing some luscious fruit in a garden, but to his dismay he could find no way to enter. At last he discovered an opening through which, he thought, if I fast three days I will be able to squeeze through. He did so; and he now feasted to his heart's delight on the grapes and all the other good things in*

the orchard. But lo! When he wanted to escape before the owner of the garden would find him, he discovered to his great distress that the opening had again become too small for him. Poor animal! Again he had to fast three days, and as he escaped, he cast a farewell glance upon the scene of his late revels saying, "O garden, charming art thou, delicious are thy fruits! But what have I now for all my labor and cunning?" So it is with man. Naked he comes into the world; naked must he leave it. After all his toil therein he carries nothing away with him except the good deeds he leaves behind.[4]

Such teaching has led many Jewish people to state simply, "I will live on through my family's memory of me." Though that thought may comfort some, it scarcely approaches the true hope found in the Bible and echoed by the voice of traditional Judaism.

In fact, the *Amidah*, a standard prayer recited in synagogues the world over, asserts, "God keeps faith with those who lie in the dust and will, according to his mercy, raise the dead, restore them bodily, and grant them eternal life."[5] This prayer was written by Rabbi Moses Ben-Maimon (Maimonides), the 12th-century Jewish philosopher and physician whose immense contribution to Judaism included the Thirteen Articles of Faith that many Orthodox Jews still adhere to today. In addition, the Talmud teaches that "all Israel has a portion in the world-to-come."[6]

Indeed, some Jewish people believe in a future resurrection. They believe it will occur when Messiah comes. Then all Jewish people will be brought back to *Eretz Yisrael*, the land of Israel. Some Hasidim (ultra-Orthodox) say resurrection is not a one-time event. Instead, it is a process called *gilful neshamot*, the turning, or rolling, of souls.[7] They believe "the souls of the righteous are reborn in the process of *tikkun olam*, the mending of the world."[8] Such a belief tries to answer questions about injustice in the world and states that *tikkun olam* cleanses the soul.

Reincarnation is alien to most Jewish people. Their most commonly held belief is that good deeds will lead to a place called *Gan Eden* (Garden of Eden, not where Adam and Eve were but a place of spiritual perfection); and continual evil will lead to *Gehinnom*, or hell. Both are found in the Talmud. *Gan Eden* is where the righteous will sit at golden tables on stools of gold, participating in lavish banquets.[9] It has been described like this: "Tables and candlesticks, thrones and crowns were there to be seen . . . they were there for the souls that were pure and clean."[10]

Gehinnom (also called *Gehenna*) is a place so awful that a single day there feels like an eternity. That is why the great Rabbi Akiba (A.D. 50–135) said the judgment of the wicked there "shall endure [only] twelve months."[11] "If one day was like an eternity, one year will be unbearable."[12]

Although much Jewish thinking focuses on rabbinic thought, we need to see what the Jewish Bible actually teaches. The Torah (five Books of Moses) uses the expression "gathered to his people" for such personages as Abraham (Gen. 25:8), Ishmael (Gen. 25:17), Isaac (Gen. 35:29), Jacob (Gen. 49:33), and Moses and Aaron (Dt. 32:50). Conversely, the sinner is "cut off from his people." This punishment is referred to as *kareit* (literally, "cutting off," but usually translated "spiritual excision"), meaning the soul loses its portion in the world to come.[13]

The word *Sheol* is used in numerous passages in the Hebrew Bible to describe the abode of the dead. *Sheol* literally means "the grave"; and from an earthly perspective, that is what it is. Yet from God's perspective, it describes a place of sorrow.[14]

In addition, the Hebrew Scriptures tell of two people whom God took alive from the earth: Enoch, who "walked with God, and he was not" (Gen. 5:24); and Elijah, who "went up by a whirlwind into heaven" in a chariot of fire (2 Ki. 2:11).

The book of Daniel provides further insight on the afterlife:

> And many of those who sleep [are dead] in the dust of
> the earth shall awake, some to everlasting life, and
> some to shame and everlasting contempt (Dan. 12:2).

Daniel did not name the two places he clearly described as heaven and hell. It is evident, however, that the first location is preferred over the second. The people there have risen from the dead to receive everlasting life, as further understood by the word *awake* (conscience), which follows the word *sleep* (death). The prophet Isaiah said,

> *Thy dead men shall live, together with my dead body*
> *shall they arise. Awake and sing, ye that dwell in dust;*
> *for thy dew is like the dew of herbs, and the earth shall*
> *cast out the dead* (Isa. 26:19).

Isaiah makes it clear that a future exists for those who have perished. Job, a contemporary of Abraham, also had a steadfast hope beyond this life when he said, "And though after my skin worms destroy this body, yet in my flesh shall I see God" (Job 19:26). Clearly, biblical Judaism holds to a strong doctrine of a defined afterlife.

I left Max's funeral with mixed emotions. I felt sad that so many educated, gifted people seemed satisfied with their uncertainty concerning life beyond the grave. I also felt sorry for the rabbi, who, for all his knowledge, could offer so little encouragement to the family.

On the other hand, I had a genuine sense of joy. You see, I knew something the rabbi did not know. I knew that Max had trusted Jesus as his Messiah. Max knew where his new home would be when death claimed his body. He had tried to tell people about his life-transforming decision and the hope he had in his heart. In fact, many of the people who attended his funeral had received a telephone call from him, telling them of his relationship with Jesus. But most, if not all of them, did not believe it. They thought the stroke had affected his mind.

But I knew differently. There was nothing wrong with Max's mind. Max had told me that he had searched a long time to find the answers about life after death. Much of that search was conducted within Judaism. I am privileged to possess many of the

Jewish books he looked to for help. But it wasn't until two former employees, both faithful, Bible-believing women, opened
the pages of the Hebrew Bible with him that he knew he had
found the truth.

So, while many still say, "when you're dead, you're dead,"
those of us who believe God's Word joyously echo Paul in
Philippians 1:21: "For to me to live is Christ, and to die is gain."
I know Max agrees.

PONDERING THE QUESTION OF EVIL

WHY IS THERE SO MUCH EVIL IN THE world? That question has challenged philosophers and scholars since time began. Spend just thirty minutes watching the national news—with its usual display of wars, man's injustice to his fellow man, murders, violent crime, and war—and it becomes obvious why so many people ask such a question.

For centuries Jewish people have pondered the question of evil. In a book titled *Understanding Judaism*, Eugene Borowitz explained sin (or evil) this way: "Judaism knows there are many influences on us. Despite them, it insists that we are free and so, responsible."[1] The book of Ben Sirach (translated into Greek about 132 B.C.) sums up the Jewish view this way:

> Don't say "God made me do evil" for God doesn't want people to be evil. . . . If you want to, you can keep the commandments. Besides, it's simple sense to do what God wants. Life and death are in front of you. You'll get what you choose.[2]

Every spring Jewish people the world over search their homes to remove all *hametz* (leaven) before they celebrate the feast of

Passover. Using a candle to provide light, a large feather to sweep up the leaven, and a large wooden spoon to collect it in, they gather the *hametz* and cast it out of their homes. This tradition binds them with their ancestors who performed the same symbolic ceremony; and it connects leaven with evil. A quote from a Passover *Haggadah* (the booklet used to direct the celebration of Passover) explains the custom: "By removing the leaven from our homes we symbolize our desire for liberation from the corrupting influences which make us subservient to our passions and evil desires."[3]

Between the two biblical feasts of *Rosh Hashanah* (the Jewish New Year) and *Yom Kippur* (Day of Atonement), Jewish people go to a moving creek or river near their homes. There they recite a prayer and cast bread (leaven) into the moving water. As the water carries the bread away, they express their desire before God that He will carry their sins far from them. This ceremony is called *Tashlich* and, like casting out the Passover leaven, is symbolic of removing sin or evil.

These unique practices in two of Israel's seven biblical feasts emphasize rabbinic Judaism's strong desire to deal with the issue of sin and its consequences.

While attending Hebrew school as a boy, I was taught that people possess two urges that battle inside them every day: the *yetzer ha-ra*, the urge to do bad, and the *yetzer ha-tov*, the urge to do good. The rabbis arrived at this position by interpreting the Hebrew word *vayyitzer* (formed) found in Genesis 2:7: "And the LORD God formed man of the dust of the ground." According to many rabbis, the two *yods* (like the English letter *y*) stand for the word *yetzer*, which means "impulse." This they believe indicates that man was created with two impulses, one good (*yetzer ha-tov*) and one evil (*yetzer ha-ra*).[4]

Judaism has long been regarded as a religion that emphasizes *mitzvot*, or good deeds. It teaches that there are 365 positive deeds and 248 negative ones, for a total of 613. A constant unction exists to strive to follow the Law. Yet the urge to disobey also is constant. Commenting on the battle of these two urges, Yehiel Mikhal, the Hasidic Rebbe of Zlotchov, put it this way: "One of the favorite tricks of the evil urge is to tell people that they really ought to be perfect. When they find they can't be they give in to the evil urge altogether."[5]

In the book *What Christians Should Know About Jews and Judaism*, Rabbi Yechiel Eckstein expressed a long-held Jewish view: "Although the rabbis regarded man as intrinsically pure, they readily acknowledged that he is in possession of both a 'good and a bad inclination.'"[6] Rabbinic Judaism does not believe in the depravity of man, as does biblical Christianity. Yet the consensus of Jewish thought is that the good impulse is not innate but, rather, comes on a person later in life. Some believe it comes gradually, growing stronger over time. Others believe it comes all at once at the time of *bar/bat mitzvah*, when, according to the rabbis, individuals become accountable for their own sins.

The *yetzer ha-ra*, the evil inclination, is likened to selfishness. A rabbinic story explains it this way: The evil inclination within man lusts only after what is forbidden. On the Day of Atonement, when eating and drinking are strictly prohibited, Rabbi Mana visited Rabbi Haggai, who was sick. Rabbi Haggai complained, "I am very thirsty."

Rabbi Manna said to him, "Seeing that you are sick, you may drink." After a while, Rabbi Mana returned and asked Rabbi Haggai, "How is your thirst?"

Rabbi Haggai replied, "The moment you permitted me to drink, my thirst disappeared."[7]

When left to run amok, unchecked by the *yetzer ha-tov*, these selfish desires can produce terrible consequences. For example, nothing is wrong with hunger; but if it leads one to steal food, it is wrong. Nothing is wrong with sexual desire; but if it leads one to commit adultery, it is wrong.

Because they believe that God formed (*vayyitzer*) man with these two urges, the rabbis contend that the *yetzer ha-ra* (evil inclination) can be a positive force. Commenting on Ecclesiastes

4:4, the Talmud states, "King Solomon taught that all labor and skillful enterprise come from men's envy of each other" (Genesis, Rabbah 9:7). The Midrash (rabbinic writings) reports that without the evil inclination, "a man would not build a house or marry or have children or engage in commerce."[8]

The idea of a fallen angel (Satan) who makes life miserable for people is not generally accepted within Judaism. Instead, Judaism teaches that people make conscious choices and are entirely responsible for which impulses they follow. However, even though Jewish people may reject the concept of Satan working in the world, the Jewish Scriptures teach it nonetheless, as demonstrated in the books of Job, Isaiah, Ezekiel, and 1 Chronicles, which clearly depict a literal Satan. His activities are described in Job 2 and Isaiah 14; his appearance is described in Ezekiel 28; and his name is given in Job 2 and 1 Chronicles 21. Yet most Jewish people say Satan is a fable used to explain the existence of evil. His description in the Bible is regarded as the personification of each person's selfish desires. Some observant Jews teach that the *yetzer ha-ra*, Satan, and the angel of death are one and the same.[9]

Judaism acknowledges the constant temptation to do what is bad, wrong, or evil. When God gave the Law to the Jewish people at Mt. Sinai, He wanted them to follow His commands. Thus Jewish people know what is right and good. They are taught to follow the *yetzer ha-tov*, the good inclination, to hate what is evil and cling to what is good. When they fail, the result is guilt.

Guilt has dominated the Jewish experience for years. In fact, it often protects Jewish individuals from yielding to the "evil urge" and pushes them to follow the good.

The Talmud addresses this subject when it comments on 2 Samuel 12:4: "The *yetzer ha-ra* is first called a passerby, then a guest and, finally, one who occupies the house. When a man sins and repeats the sin, it no longer seems to him as forbidden" (Yoma 88b).

How does Judaism deal with the whole sin issue? Most Jewish people would say they deal with sin once a year during

Yom Kippur when they spend an entire day in the synagogue, fasting and praying. Therein lies a fundamental difference between modern Judaism and biblical Christianity.

Bible-believing Christians consider every word of the Holy Scriptures to be the Word of God—including, of course, the Old Testament. Thus creation, the flood, and the tower of Babel are actual, historical events. Equally as true is the account of satanic temptation and the fall of man, recorded in Genesis 3. The Bible says Adam and Eve disobeyed God and ate of the forbidden fruit. Their disobedience to God's command changed them and their progeny forever. The Bible also says that God created man in His own image and that, after the fall, "Adam lived an hundred and thirty years, and begot a son in *his own likeness*, after *his image*; and called his name Seth" (Gen. 5:3, italics added). To be sure, Seth possessed remnants of God's image; but when his father, Adam, had sinned, God's image within man became marred. Christians believe that human beings, beginning with Adam, pass this marred image of God to every child who is born. Jewish Scripture supports the concept that every person is born with a sin nature and is not innately good but, rather, utterly depraved: "The heart is deceitful above all things, and desperately wicked; who can know it?" (Jer. 17:9). "And God saw that the wickedness of man was great in the earth, and that every imagination of the thoughts of his heart was only evil continually" (Gen. 6:5). Such was the consequence of Adam's sin.

Why is there so much evil in the world? Because the human heart is "desperately wicked." Jesus understood the real meaning of *leaven* when He commented on the hard-heartedness of many of the Pharisees. He wanted His disciples to ponder the question of evil and, as they did so, to consider the only true cure for human depravity—Him:

> Who his own self bore our sins in his own body on the tree, that we, being dead to sins, should live unto righteousness; by whose stripes ye were healed (1 Pet. 2:24).

TIKKUN OLAM

It is our duty to praise the Lord of all things, to ascribe greatness to Him who formed the world in the beginning, since He hath not made us like the nations of other lands, and hath not placed us like other families of the earth, since He hath not assigned unto us a portion as unto them, nor a lot as unto all their multitude.

For we bend the knee and offer worship and thanks before the supreme King of kings, the Holy One, blessed be He.

Who stretched forth the heavens and laid the foundations of the earth, the seat of whose glory is in the heavens above, and the abode of whose might is in the loftiest heights. He is our God; there is none else: in truth He is our King; there is none besides Him; as it is written in His Law, And thou shalt know this day, and lay it to thine heart, that the Lord He is God in heaven above and upon the earth beneath; there is none else.[1]

"IS IT ALMOST OVER?" WHO HASN'T SAT in a meeting without thinking such a thing? For those who regularly attend "religious" worship services, the question probably has not only been thought, but spoken as well. Although it was not by design, there is within Jewish liturgy a prayer that tells the worshiper when "over" is approaching. The prayer, quoted in part above, is called *Aleinu le-shabbeah*—"It is our duty to praise." Most Jewish people know it simply as *Aleinu*. Its familiar melody and words are always chanted near the end of the prayers that are recited three times a day. It is also placed near the end of the New Year (*Rosh Hashanah*) service.

Composed in the third century A.D., *Aleinu* was used in the Middle Ages whenever Jews were martyred. The theme of the prayer "is the kingdom of God."[2] Contained within the first paragraph of the worship poem are offerings of praise to God for His creative power and His choice of the Jewish people as His own. With the second paragraph, worshipers bend their knees before Him. The third paragraph praises His glory and the fact that "there is none besides Him." And the fourth paragraph speaks of Jewish hope that rests in Him to remove various abominations and idols from the world.

Contained within the fourth paragraph is a phrase that reads, *when the world will be perfected under the kingdom of the Almighty.* While meditating on the prayer, sixteenth-century Kabbalist (mystic) Isaac Luria was moved to deep study. He wrestled with the prayer's three basic concepts: God's sovereign selection of the Jewish people, God's creative power, and the perfection attained under God's kingdom.

Trapping the 'Divine Light'

Although he is among the lesser-known rabbis, Luria's conclusions have immensely influenced juristic thought to this day. Luria came up with a story to explain the condition of the world and to provide hope in dealing with it. In Luria's story God had several vessels that contained His essence or light. A heavenly calamity occurred when an explosion caused "divine light" particles to come into contact with evil matter. Writer Joseph Naft explained that, according to Luria, "Our world consists of countless shards of the original vessels entrapping sparks of the Divine light. Humanity's great task involves helping God by freeing and reuniting the scattered light."[3] The prevailing thought among extremely observant Jews at that time was, "By obeying the commandments and living pious lives, Jews could help free the divine sparks and repair the broken universe."[4] Such thinking resulted in the concept and resultant phrase *tikkun olam*, or "repairing the world." The term, wrote Francine Klagsbrun in *Moment* magazine, "has become synonymous in Jewish life with acts of social justice, which, for many Jews have come to stand for all of Judaism."[5]

This rabbinic ordinance was made for the good of society. Observant Jews today use the phrase to encourage people to perform *mitzvot* (commandments) to "help" God make things right. The Talmud states, "It is not upon you to finish the work, but you are not free to ignore it (Mishna, Ethics, 2:21)."[6]

Bettering the world is not to be a one-time effort. It is a process: "In order to be a partner with G-d, there has to be a connection. Just as one prepares for the day ahead, and just as you must spend 'quality' time with your spouse in order to keep the vitality in your marriage, one also needs to look at one's relationship with G-d."[7]

For some observant Jews, one way to "fix the world" is through repentance. Rabbi Abraham Kook, the first Ashkenazi chief rabbi of Israel, taught that repentance would help bring about the healing of creation. Other observant Jewish leaders emphasize that repairing the world takes place when one strives to become observant and live a Jewish lifestyle.

Although the more observant Jews birthed the concept of *tikkun olam*, it was the Reform Jewish movement that embraced it and expanded it. "It was the giants of the early Reform movement who took this idea of *'repairing the world'* and told us how to do it," says Rabbi Margaret Holub.[8] They did so by tweaking the idea of "repairing" into simply making the world a better place to live in. Many organizations are dedicated to such humanitarian causes as feeding the hungry, improving race relations, instituting social justice (organizations fighting social injustice), women's rights, etc.

There is even a *tikkun olam* award. A two-time winner of the award is Peter Yarrow of the once-popular singing group Peter, Paul, and Mary.

These overtures can indeed be helpful, even noble. But in reality they have little, if any, relationship with Judaism. Yet these organizations refer to the "Jewish teaching, *tikkun olam.*"

CUOMO-LIEBERMAN PHILOSOPHIES

The idea of *tikkun olam* has even entered the political arena. In the United States two liberal Democrats—one Jewish, one Gentile—invoke a *tikkun olam* philosophy in their lifestyles. The first is former New York Governor Mario Cuomo. In an interview with journalist Jack Newfield, Cuomo, calling himself a Christian, reportedly said the following:

> *Tikkun olam, translated roughly, means to repair or cure the universe. What it means to me as a Christian—because it was a truth adopted by Christianity as a cardinal principle—is that God made the world but did not finish it, and our mission as individuals is to use all of our strength to finish the world, to complete it, making it as good a place as we can. That is the mission that gives our life significance. We are perceived, as Christians, as an army trying to win the battle against imperfection.*[9]

Although Cuomo may have a handle on the meaning of *tikkun olam*, he sorely missed the mark when it comes to understanding biblical Christianity. The Bible teaches that God created a perfect world and man ruined it with sin. Furthermore, man has absolutely no ability whatsoever to "repair" it. God Himself will do so when He creates the new heavens and new earth.

Sen. Joe Lieberman of Connecticut, a failed vice presidential candidate and former presidential hopeful, is an observant Jew who says he has been greatly influenced by the idea of *tikkun olam*:

> "The summary of our aspirations was in the Hebrew phrase tikkun olam, which is translated 'to improve the world' or more boldly to complete the creation which God began. . . . my faith was just one of many great gifts my father and mother, Henry and Marcia Lieberman, gave me," wrote Joe Lieberman in his recent political autobiography, In Praise of Public Life (Simon and Shuster [sic], New York, 2000).[10]

SINCERE BUT FLAWED

Although belief in *tikkun olam* may inspire people to do good works, help their fellowman, and work diligently to make the world a better place, the concept, nevertheless, is not found anywhere in the Jewish Scriptures. The idea of helping God fix the world is entirely manmade, appealing to the well-intentioned but misinformed. It also can lead to further error. Rabbi Margaret Holub wrote:

> I don't really think we are God's partners in repairing the world. I think we are the whole show—with all our confusion, all our limitations, all our misguided passions, all the diversions, all the disinformation. If anything, maybe God provides the cry, the call. But if we don't respond, no one will, I'm afraid.[11]

I recently asked a Jewish woman if she had heard of *tikkun olam*. Her reply was that not only had she heard of it, it was all she heard about at her synagogue until that rabbi left. "He centered all the work around *tikkun olam*," she said, "helping God perfect the world."

The *Aleinu* prayer is the source behind the idea of *tikkun olam*. How sad it is that Rabbi Luria interpreted the words *the world will be perfected under the kingdom of the Almighty* to mean human beings would do the perfecting instead of God Himself. Sadder still is the fact that the Hebrew Scriptures do not teach *tikkun olam*. In fact, they teach that God is perfect and righteous and mankind is sinful and unrighteous. It is not God who needs help. It is we who do.

And two thousand years ago, on an old rugged cross, God gave us the greatest help we would ever receive. He provided a final atonement for our sins so that we could be "perfected" by faith:

> *Surely he hath borne our griefs, and carried our sorrows; yet we did esteem him stricken, smitten of God, and afflicted. But he was wounded for our transgressions, he was bruised for our iniquities; the chastisement for our peace was upon him, and with his stripes we are healed* (Isa. 53:4–5).

THE TATTOO IS TABOO

OUR NEIGHBORHOOD BOASTED A PENNY candy store ingeniously located on my route to school. In addition to the tempting and inexpensive candy, one of the most popular items in the store was the individualized tattoo. The shopper had a choice of several different kinds of these water-soluble tattoos. Animals, superheroes, and cartoon characters were just a few of the varieties. They were easily applied to the body. First, the wrapper was carefully opened, then the location of the tattoo was determined and moistened, whereupon the tattoo was held on the area for a few minutes. Then, voila! Instant tattoo!

I must admit that my parents were not taken with the idea of their children displaying colored pictures on their arms and legs, although they tolerated our whims. From time to time, I felt it necessary to defend my using them. I didn't think it was such a big deal because, after all, they were not permanent. My father would respond by telling me about his war days and the many men he knew who acquired real tattoos. He impressed upon me that real tattoos are painful to have put on, don't come off (easily, that is), and can quickly go out of date. Then my mother would chime in with the final argument: "Jewish people don't do those things to their bodies—voluntarily" (undoubtedly a reference to the Holocaust, when the Nazis forced millions of Jewish people to bear numbers tattooed on their hands or stomachs).

Today my parents see a lot more than removable tattoos on children. They see young people making fashion statements by displaying real tattoos, piercing their bodies in peculiar places, and dying or shaving their heads. These things have left my parents somewhat bewildered, wondering if they have become outdated models.

The truth is, there's nothing new under the sun! These phenomena are not recent at all, the new invention of some cutting-edge fashion guru. These things have existed for thousands of years, and Judaism—biblical (that which is spoken about in the Bible) and rabbinical (that which the rabbis teach)—has been teaching against them.

People groups as far back as the ancient Egyptians have marked their bodies with tattoos, crooked marks cut into their skin, and shaven heads—much of it as part of pagan ritualistic worship. The Torah stands against such things, as the Lord specified to Moses in the Law, clearly stating, "Ye shall not shave around your temples; neither shalt thou mar the corners of thy beard. Ye shall not make any cuttings in your flesh for the dead, nor tattoo any marks upon you: I am the Lord" (Lev. 19:27–28). Deuteronomy 14:1 further warns against cutting the body, a practice the 450 false prophets of Baal performed as they competed with Elijah to determine whose God was more powerful.

There are other fashion statements that would not be embraced by Orthodox Judaism. One is shaven heads. Men are forbidden to shave their heads because it is outlawed in Leviticus 21:5. Hasidic women, on the other hand, do shave their heads. This takes place upon marriage and is based on Deuteronomy 21:12, interpreted as a change in a woman's status from single to married.[1] After an observant Jewess marries and shears her head, she would never dream of exposing it in public. A woman with an exposed shorn head would bring shame upon herself. The public display of a woman's shorn head is associated with cultic practices long ago carried out by pagan temple prostitutes. To maintain their modesty, Hasidic women wear wigs or cloth head coverings.

Also forbidden is body piercing; and men must not dye their hair, as specified in Leviticus 19 and in the rabbinical interpretation of Deuteronomy 22:5. The rabbis forbid men to identify with anything that has feminine connotations.

There are further commands by God that set His chosen people apart from others. Hasidic males grow long locks on the "corners" of their heads. These distinctive, thick tufts of hair are called *payot*. In addition, many Jewish men grow beards, which are regarded by the sages and scholars as a sign of maturity and piety.

Maimonides cited five specific areas of the face that are not to be shaved. They are both sides of the head by the ears, both sides of the chin, and the peak of the chin. Knowing the Orthodox Jewish position on this issue provides a compassionate insight into the degradation that bearded Jewish men must have suffered during World War II when the Nazis forced many to be shaved in public.

Another distinction of the Orthodox Jewish male is the use of a head covering. While Gentile propriety is demonstrated by a man's removing his hat upon entering a building or in the presence of a lady, Jewish teaching compels men to demonstrate respect to God at all times by keeping their heads covered.

Old Testament Scripture teaches that the high priest had his head covered as part of his special attire. This covering, called a *miter*, was probably a wrap-type cloth that went around his head, similar to a turban. In his book *The Jewish Book of Why*, Alfred Kolatch quotes Babylonian talmudic scholar Huna ben Joshua, who said, "I never walked four cubits with uncovered head because God dwells over my head."[2] Yet there is no scriptural reference to a man, other than the high priest, covering his head.

In the ancient world, Roman citizens had their heads uncovered, while all Roman slaves had their heads covered. In keeping with Judaism's teaching of distinctiveness and separation, many Jewish men believe there is greater piety when the head is covered. "Cover your head so that the reverence of Heaven be upon you."[3] Thus the head covering became part of Judaism around the fifth century A.D., serving as a reminder that God reigns above man at all times. This covering is called by different names. In English, it is called a *skullcap*; in Hebrew, a *kippah*. It is probably best known by the Yiddish word *yarmulke*.

Today Jewish people are debating whether or not a head covering is required at all. Orthodox men are still required to cover their heads at all times, while men in Conservative congregations use head coverings only at their services. Reform Jews require no head covering at all. In many synagogues, extra *yarmulkes* are made available for men who arrive without them. In Israel at the holy sites, cardboard *yarmulkes* are handed out so that all men may show the respect due in such auspicious places.

In our age of high visibility, there seems to be an invasion of *body degraders*. It should be clearly understood that these issues have been dealt with from a Jewish—particularly an Orthodox Jewish—point of view. Believers are not under the Law but are under grace. The New Testament makes it clear that the Law is holy, just, and good (Rom. 7:12). It also clearly states that the body is the temple of the Holy Spirit. It behooves us, therefore, to view fashion with a discerning eye. Let us all be on guard for any compromise of our bodies, which house our eternal beings.

ORGANIZED FOR SERVICE

IN 1843 TWELVE JEWISH MEN, EACH one an immigrant, met on the Lower East Side of New York City. Their purpose was to form an organization to help their own people in need—a type of mutual-aid society. The work they began has endured for more than 150 years, and today the B'nai B'rith (Children of the Covenant) is the oldest service organization among the Jewish people.

Its mission statement appears at the beginning of its constitution:

> *B'nai B'rith has taken upon itself the mission of uniting persons of the Jewish faith in the work of promoting their highest interests and those of humanity; of developing and elevating the mental and moral character of the people of our faith; of inculcating the purest principles of philanthropy, honor, and patriotism; of supporting science and art; alleviating the wants of the poor and needy; visiting and attending the sick; coming to the rescue of victims of persecution; providing for, and protecting, and assisting the widow and orphan on the broadest principle of humanity.*[1]

Organizing for service has long characterized the fabric of Jewish life. Even in the Bible we see how Moses organized the Israelites according to tribes (Num. 2:2). King David organized the Levites into twenty-four groups for spiritual ministry (1 Chr. 25:6ff.). And in the early church, which was almost exclusively Jewish, the apostles set apart seven men to minister to the physical needs of that newborn body (Acts 6).

Throughout the world, Jewish people continue to form organizations for service. Some care for religious and spiritual needs while others minister to the physical and social needs of the Jewish people.

B'nai B'rith's comprehensive mission statement has served it well over the years and has helped guide and focus its work. The ravages of the Civil War in America had left many Jewish children without parents. B'nai B'rith established an orphanage in Cleveland, Ohio; and the leadership of B'nai B'rith helped prevent the expulsion of Jews from some southern states.[2]

In 1865 B'nai B'rith contributed to the aid of people suffering from cholera in what is today Israel. When a fire devastated the city of Chicago in 1871, B'nai B'rith provided food, clothes, and medical supplies.[3] At the turn of the twentieth century, when Jewish immigration to the United States was at its peak, B'nai B'rith was there to organize and assist.

B'nai B'rith has always kept pace with the needs of the people, creating simple but effective outreaches called societies. Coal societies provided coal for families who could not afford to heat their homes. Matzoh societies provided matzoh for Jews who could not afford to purchase it for Passover. Loan societies made money available—interest free—to those in financial need.[4] From these emerged more extensive endeavors to help clothe the poor, feed the hungry, aid victims of such disasters as hurricanes, and help survivors of tragedies like the 1995 bombing of the federal building in Oklahoma City.[5]

Education has also been part of B'nai B'rith's vision. One of its first projects was to build Covenant Hall in New York City, a forerunner of what we know today as the Jewish Community Center (JCC). Completed in 1851, it housed Maimonides Library, which was used as a Jewish public library.[6]

Educating future generations of Jewish youth has always been a major concern for many Jewish leaders. To address that issue, B'nai B'rith organized B'nai B'rith Youth Organization (B.B.Y.O.) in 1923. Chapters were started all across the country, consisting of B.B.G. (B'nai B'rith Girls) and A.Z.A. (Aleph Zadic Alef) for boys.

As a teenager, I participated in A.Z.A. Our chapter was called David, after the Israelite king. As required, an adult volunteer served as our leader and advisor. Each chapter was bound by national guidelines that outlined the various activities we could participate in. Our chapter was involved in community enrichment, fund-raising for Israel, nursing home visitation, and social and religious activities. These activities gave us a sense of pride, both as Jews and Americans. Today approximately 30,000 high school-aged people are involved in B.B.Y.O.[7]

Born from its desire to continue to work with students after their high school years, B'nai B'rith formed the Hillel organization to work among the college aged. Hillel first made itself available to the 400 Jewish students at the University of Illinois in 1923. Since then it has grown into the largest international Jewish campus organization in the world.

Since Bible times, persecution has been a fact of life for the Jewish people. So B'nai B'rith set up the Anti-Defamation League in 1913 to protect the Jewish people whenever they are attacked or slandered.[8] Today many regard the ADL as the leading advocate in the fight against anti-Semitism in the United States.

Most Jewish people have always highly valued education, but they often were barred from admission to institutions of higher learning simply because they were Jewish. In 1880 a group of Jewish Russians received permission from the czar to start agricultural schools to train and feed Russia's five million Jews living in poverty. The Society for Trades and Agricultural Labor was established, known the world over as ORT, the acronym for its Russian name, Obschestvo Remeslenovoi Zemledelcheskovo Trouda.[9]

For the next twenty-five years, in spite of an anti-Semitic Russian government, ORT successfully trained 25,000 Jews in 350 towns. After World War I, ORT expanded into other Eastern European countries. Each chapter established trade schools to train people for skilled jobs. A branch was opened in Brooklyn, New York, in 1927. Soviet dictator Joseph Stalin shut ORT down in the Soviet Union in 1938; but fifty-two years later, with the collapse of Communism, it was revived in that country. Today the countries of the former Soviet Union have twenty-two ORT schools that provide much-needed technical training.[10]

In 1948, in the fledgling State of Israel, ORT opened a school in Tel-Aviv. At least 100,000 Jewish, Arab, and Druze students today attend 140 schools and colleges in fifty-three communities. ORT is a nonsectarian and nonpolitical organization that oversees a global network of schools teaching more than 280,000 students in more than sixty countries.[11]

Of all the many Jewish organizations around the world, Hadassah is perhaps the most familiar one. To appreciate Hadassah's contribution to modern society, listen to these words of Scripture, read at the memorial of Hadassah's founder, Henrietta Szold:

> *I was eyes to the blind, and feet was I to the lame. I was*
> *a father to the poor; and the cause which I knew not I*
> *searched out. And I broke the jaws of the wicked, and*
> *plucked the prey out of his teeth* (Job 29:15–17).[12]

Daughter of a Baltimore rabbi, Henrietta Szold associated herself with the Daughters of Zion, a group of women interested in the establishment of a homeland for the Jewish people. She became appalled at the living conditions in Palestine when she visited there in 1912. Disease was rampant and sanitary conditions poor for both Arabs and Jews. Shortages of doctors, nurses, and hospitals exacerbated the situation.

When Henrietta Szold returned to the United States, she almost immediately began a new chapter of the Daughters of Zion. Calling it Hadassah after the Hebrew name of Queen Esther in the Bible, she embarked on a mission to raise money to send medical supplies and personnel to help the Palestinian Jews and Arabs. These women met regularly at Temple Emanu-El in New York City. In the first year, they raised $930. In 1913 the chapter sent two American public health nurses to begin a maternity center that also treated children with trachoma.[13] In 1918 forty-four physicians, nurses, sanitary engineers, dentists, and administrative staff set sail for Palestine. The money was gathered with the help and sponsorship of Hadassah and the Joint Distribution Committee.[14]

Hadassah's crowning achievement, however, came in 1939 with the completion of a hospital bearing its name on Mt. Scopus in Jerusalem. Yet fewer than ten years later, in 1948 during the Israeli War of Independence, tragedy struck when the Arabs massacred seventy-eight doctors and nurses as their medical bus passed through an Arab neighborhood en route to the hospital. From 1948 to 1967, the hospital found itself situated in an Arab-controlled area and was virtually cut off from the rest of Israel.

Ein Kerim, a new medical facility, was begun and completed on the west side of Jerusalem. Today Ein Kerim is a 700-bed facility that serves as a hospital and research facility dealing with bone marrow transplants; heart, lung, and liver transplants; laparoscopic surgery; cold laser surgery; and gene therapy.[15] The Hadassah Hospital at Mt. Scopus now has 300 beds and serves both Jews and Arabs.

An advertisement for Hadassah appeared in the October 2000 issue of *The Jerusalem Report*, an international magazine. It summarized the function of the organization, now 300,000 women strong. "With hundreds of Hadassah-sponsored programs in Israel, ranging from health care to education, youth at risk, and land development, the proud volunteers of Hadassah have chosen this year, 5761, to rededicate ourselves to the Jewish state, the Jewish people and the Jewish future."[16]

Interestingly, The Friends of Israel Gospel Ministry was also organized to serve the Jewish people. Begun as a relief society to help Jewish people fleeing Nazi persecution in 1938, The Friends of Israel has maintained a friendship with Israel and the Jewish people for more than sixty years, and we still send various forms of aid when it is needed. Although we are an evangelical Christian organization, we are, nonetheless, unequivocally committed to helping and supporting Jewish people and their biblical, God-given right to live in the land given to their forefathers.

These are but a few of the many fine Jewish organizations that were organized for service and have benefited countless numbers of people—both Jewish and Gentile—over the years.

Another great organization is Workmen's Circle.

WORKMEN'S CIRCLE

THE CHILDREN OF ISRAEL PROVIDED an interesting name for the heavenly bread sent to them from the Lord. They called it *manna*, which means "What is it?" (Ex. 16:15). The same question is asked today when people hear the name of an organization called Workmen's Circle. Despite a national membership of about twenty thousand, most Jewish people, like their wandering brethren of the past, wonder, "What is it?"

The name was familiar in my household, but as a youngster I could never really grasp what the organization was all about. I knew it was a Jewish association to which some of my family belonged. If I asked about it, the only answer I ever got was, "It is *not* Communist!" That was certainly good news. But the organization has much more going for it than the mere fact it isn't Communist.

Workmen's Circle was started more than a hundred years ago by Yiddish-speaking Jewish immigrants who were trying to make America their home. My Uncle Sam was a committed member for more than fifty years, devoting countless evenings to serving on many of the different organizational committees. He also offered his carpentry skills free of charge when they were needed for any of the many Workmen's Circle projects. When he passed away eighteen years ago, there was no question that my aunt would maintain the $75 yearly membership fee. Her reasons to do so were many, not the least of which was that, upon her death, she would be assured of being buried next to her husband in a Workmen's Circle cemetery. That is one of the many benefits of being a member in good standing, and it brings my aunt much comfort. Nor is she alone. For more than a hundred years the attraction to Circle membership has been the security its many benefits provide.

Workmen's Circle began on the Lower East Side of New York City in 1892. It was nationalized in 1900, holding its first convention in 1901. By 1905 the organization had grown to 6,776 members. That number increased dramatically to 45,666 by 1913 and just twelve years later reached its all-time high of 87,000. What moved so many in such a short time to become so attracted to this organization?

THE GOLDENAH MEDINAH

Most, if not all, of the Circle's early members were socialists. That fact is not surprising since they had come largely from Eastern European countries where terrible anti-Semitism afflicted them night and day. Eventually it drove them out and brought them to the United States.

In Russia, where Jewish people were ruthlessly slaughtered in government-sanctioned persecutions called pogroms, socialism seemed far more attractive than the brutal rule of the czar. Workmen's Circle (in Yiddish, *Der Arbeter Ring*) began in the midst of the largest immigration of Jewish people to the United States. Some two million Jews made the difficult journey between 1883 and 1917.

After arriving in America, they were processed through Ellis Island off the shores of New York City. Then many boarded nearby trains and set out for other parts of the country. There they hoped to realize their dreams in what they called in Yiddish, the *goldenah medinah*—the "golden land."

Thousands, however, stayed in New York City, daring to dream there. For most, life in the *goldenah medinah* turned out to be a struggle for survival in the tenements of New York City. To survive in a new country with a new language and few resources was difficult. But these Jews, most of them young, brought two strong convictions with them from the Old Country. First, as secular socialists, they were freethinking and tough but possessed enough humility to realize survival meant working together. Second, they were fiercely determined to maintain their Jewish identity.

Dr. Emanuel S. Goldstein, professor of Yiddish at Queens College, stated it this way: "The real raison d'etre of Workmen's Circle became the fight against assimilation."[1] Yiddish, the language of most Jews in Europe, became the language of most Jews in Workmen's Circle. At first they used it almost exclusively. Their slogan, *"a shenere un besere velt"*—"a more beautiful and better world"—nicely characterized the organization's purpose. In the words of its current president, Robert Kestenbaum,

> The essence of the Workmen's Circle/Arbeter Ring's dedication to Jewish community, Yiddish culture and social justice is not simply a tag line printed on a letterhead. Rather, it is a way of life and the fundamental reason we and others like us exist. The pursuit of a shenere un besere velt, *a better and more beautiful world, serves as a call for all to adopt in their own way to fulfill personal and collective responsibilities.*[2]

With an understood objective of providing mutual aid and assistance to those of like mind and circumstance, Workmen's Circle provided the additional benefits of camaraderie and friendship. Membership brought people together. Before networking became a familiar business term, members of the Circle did it, not to get ahead but because it was a good thing. As a result, membership increased rapidly.

SOCIAL SERVICES

Cash gifts. The life of a new immigrant was difficult. Even if it was only a few dollars, a monetary gift was an incredible help to a stranger starting off in America. Many Jewish people can tell you how a $5 or $10 bill donated from the Circle gave them their start.

Union Involvement. When immigrants arrived in America they needed jobs. In those days working conditions were poor; the hours, long; the pay, low. There were no laws or unions protecting workers against employers who wished to take advantage of them. With its strong commitment to labor, Workmen's Circle worked to end sweatshops, organizing when it became necessary and even boycotting businesses when expedient to apply the financial pressure needed to change conditions. In many cases this pressure worked. To this day, the Circle still works hard to support labor and social justice.

Medical Care. Today most people have access to medical care, which is almost regarded as a national right. In the early days of the Circle, it established medical clinics for its members. Thousands of people used them for decades. When these clinics finally were forced to close because of finances, the Circle offered health insurance in their stead. For the many who have benefited from this program, "a better and more beautiful world" became a reality.

Homes for the Aged. Who among us does not have a concern about the senior season of life? It can become an overwhelming consideration. Workmen's Circle makes it possible to alleviate that concern. Its homes for the aged have met a tremendous need over the years.

Cemeteries. Workmen's Circle provides cemetery plots for members—like my aunt and uncle.

Education. Jewish immigrants brought with them a respect and desire for good education. For more than seventy-five years the I. L. Peretz schools have helped children "establish kinship with their Eastern European culture and Jewish people worldwide."[3] These schools, called *shuln* in Yiddish, offer a wide range of subjects. In fact, they constitute "the largest network of Jewish secular schools in the United States."[4] They reached their peak enrollment in 1950 with 38,000 Jewish students.

Existing all across the country, these schools have high standards and a demanding curriculum. Originally teaching almost exclusively in Yiddish, today they emphasize *Yiddishkite* (Jewish culture), which they believe will help Jewish children stay close to their roots. Although enrollment has declined over the years, several thousand students still attend these schools nationally, with about 550 in New York City alone.

Adult education classes also are offered to help expand minds as well as opportunities in America. And no education would be complete without good books. Workmen's Circle boasts a unique collection of Yiddish-language and other Jewish books, as well as reference works designed for serious study in Jewish history, literature, and culture. Appointments can be made to access the collection. Members receive a regular mailing from the Circle, which recommends books the leadership feels will enhance quality of life for its people.

CULTURAL ACTIVITIES

In addition to operating schools during the academic year, Workmen's Circle also operates camps called *Kinder Rings* to provide children with wholesome recreation during the summer and foster a sense of pride in their identity as Jews.

Cultural pursuits historically have been important in the lives of the Jewish people. Workmen's Circle still promotes *Folksbiene* (Yiddish theatre).

It also has provided many opportunities for its members to access the kinds of entertainment that will not only entertain but tap into the rich heritage of the Jewish people. The organization's Web site states, "Singing timeless melodies in Yiddish and other songs known to Jews throughout the world, our choruses perpetuate our legacy as they expand their musical repertoires."[5] During the summer season Yiddish folksongs are performed publicly in parks where no admission is charged.

Workmen's Circle has been a great help to the Jewish community. Consistent with the Torah's commandment, "Thou shalt love thy neighbor as thyself" (Lev. 19:18), Workmen's Circle has provided members with mutual aid and health and death benefits and has aligned itself with Jewish unions in an effort to help working-class Jewish people. It also has aligned itself with a Yiddish newspaper (*The Forward*) in an effort to inform and educate.

Christians can glean a great deal from humanitarian organizations like this one so that we can minister to people of like precious faith. Providing a measure of security for people is a good thing. But dependency on people must never supersede dependence on God. My aunt has maintained her membership in Workmen's Circle for many years and is thrilled to know that someday she will lie next to her husband in their Workmen's Circle plot. More important, however, is the fact that many years ago, at eighty years of age, she placed her faith in her Messiah for the security of an eternal place in heaven.

POLITICS AND POLITICIANS

FROM THE TIME OF ISRAEL'S INCEPTION as a modern state in 1948, the United States has been its consistent and loyal friend. In our country, many issues seem to be based on political affiliation. The treatment of Israel, so far at least, has not been one of those issues.

Historically, the American/Jewish population has voted Democratic. Our family was no exception. In fact, I can't recall anyone in my old neighborhood who voted Republican. In our home, the names of Roosevelt and Kennedy were spoken with almost the same reverence as the biblical names of Moses and David. I can remember my mother telling me that she believed the Democrats understood our people better than the Republicans. While that statement is certainly inaccurate, it is true that most Jewish people are politically liberal.

Interestingly, both Republicans and Democrats have served as U.S. presidents since the birth of the State of Israel. I believe it is safe to say that Israel has benefited from all of them. In the early years of Israel's modern history, two American presidents—one Democrat and one Republican—set the pattern for America's friendly relations with the Jewish state.

HARRY S. TRUMAN

Harry S. Truman, the Democrat, was the 33rd president of the United States. Known for the slogan, "The buck stops here," Truman went against the counsel of his advisors and the desire of many in the State Department and recognized Israel's status as a nation on May 14, 1948. That recognition came just eleven minutes after Israel's first prime minister, David Ben Gurion, made the announcement of statehood. I believe three factors contributed to Truman's action. First, Truman was a Bible reader, having read through the Scriptures three times by the time he was thirteen. Second, he had great sympathy for the Jewish people, especially those who had suffered through the Holocaust. Third, and most important, he had maintained a friendship with a Jewish man named Eddie Jacobson from his days in World War I.

During the war, Captain Truman was made regimental canteen officer. Having no business experience, he selected Jacobson, who had been a traveling salesman before the war, to be his manager. The two men worked well together and were successful in operating these military social clubs. After the war, they decided to go into business for themselves and opened a haberdashery called Truman and Jacobson. The store was quite successful until a severe recession forced them out of business in 1921. Then they split up to pursue their own interests but remained friends throughout their lives.

Truman went on to serve as county judge in Jackson County, Missouri, for several years, followed by two terms as U.S. senator from Missouri. In 1944, he was elected vice president on the presidential ticket with Franklin Roosevelt. The death of President Roosevelt on April 12, 1945, elevated Truman to the highest office in the land.

With evidence emerging daily of the horrors of the Holocaust, Truman acted as an advocate for homeless Jews. He petitioned the British government to allow a hundred thousand displaced Jews from Germany and Austria to be admitted to Palestine, but his request was refused. On the Day of Atonement, Yom Kippur 1946, he delivered a speech to Congress asking for an increase in immigration into the United States to accommodate many displaced Jews. Calls for a Jewish state were on the rise, and so was the pressure for Truman to stay clear of the issue.

In March 1948, Chaim Weizman, a prominent Zionist leader, flew to Washington hoping to meet with President Truman. However, Truman succumbed to political pressure and refused the meeting. It was then that Eddie Jacobson decided to pay a visit to the White House to see his old business partner. Truman was glad to see Eddie but not at all anxious to talk about Palestine. Jacobson reminded Truman of his longtime hero, Andrew Jackson, and compared him to Weizman. Jacobson said, "I have never met the man who has been my hero all my life, but I have studied his deeds, as you have studied those of Jackson. He is a statesman and a gentleman. He is an old man and a very sick man. He has traveled thousands of miles to talk to you, and you are refusing to see him. Harry, this isn't like you." President Truman decided to meet with Weizman and talked with him for more than an hour.

Two months later, the opportunity came to recognize the State of Israel. Harry Truman seized the moment, and history was made. About a year after that historic occasion, Weizman, then president of Israel, came to the United States to formally thank president Truman. He presented Truman with an Israeli Torah as a token of Israel's appreciation. He told Truman that being president of Israel was a more important job than being president of the United States. The reason, he said, was because the U.S. president presides over only 170 million people, while the president of Israel must preside over one million presidents!

To honor Truman, Polish immigrants established a *moshav* (cooperative settlement) in Israel in 1949. Kefar Truman is still functioning today.

So God indeed used a Democrat to assist in the birth of the nation.

DWIGHT D. EISENHOWER

Meanwhile, after a distinguished military career spanning more than thirty years, former General Dwight David Eisenhower, a Republican, became the 34th president of the United States.

Because of his name, many people thought Eisenhower himself was Jewish, while others accused him of being anti-Semitic. He was, in fact, raised in a Bible-believing Protestant home and had high regard for the Jewish people, acknowledging them as the chosen ones. It was while he served as supreme commander of allied forces in Europe that the Nazi concentration camps were liberated. Having heard about these camps, Eisenhower decided to view them firsthand. He said, "The same day I saw my first horror camp, I visited every nook and cranny. I felt it my duty to be in a position from then on to learn about these things in case there ever grew up those who said it was just propaganda."

General Eisenhower made the unprecedented appointment of Rabbi Judah Nadich as his special advisor on Jewish affairs. This post helped to speed up the process of dealing with the hundreds of thousands of Jewish displaced persons. While attending a Yom Kippur service at one of the displaced persons camps, he told the crowd that the American army was there to help them and that he understood their suffering. He also said that he believed a sunnier day was coming for them. He was given a standing ovation. Rabbi Nadich later wrote an article, published in the *American Zionist* magazine, stating that General Eisenhower had played a major role in saving the lives of tens of thousands of Jewish refugees during and after World War II.

All of these events played a role in the many decisions that President Eisenhower made regarding Israel. He authorized the expenditure of hundreds of millions of dollars in grants-in-aid to the new State of Israel. Included in the package were aircraft, spare parts, and ammunition. His approval of an atomic energy agreement made it possible to train Israeli scientists.

Throughout his two terms, he pledged and provided for the continued support of Israel.

So God used a Republican to help the young Israeli nation by providing the resources necessary for it to protect itself.

"I will bless them that bless thee [Israel], and curse him that curseth thee" (Gen. 12:3). That is not a political platform for either the Republicans or the Democrats. For more than fifty years so far, through the administrations of numerous presidents, God has blessed the United States as the nation has blessed His people. As political winds change, let us pray that the wind will continue to blow favorably on the Holy Land and the descendants of Abraham, Isaac, and Jacob.

AKIVA:
ASCENSION TO PROMINENCE

JOSEPH AKIVA IS KNOWN BY JEWISH people around the world as the famous Rabbi Akiva. Though he lived from A.D. 50 to 135, he is deeply revered among Jews today for his amazing insights and knowledge of Torah. He attracted such a huge following that he became known as "one of the fathers of the world."[1] His style of teaching through storytelling is so much admired today that rabbis still quote him often.

Rabbi Akiva undoubtedly rose to prominence for many reasons. However, three in particular stand out: his humility; his response to the help he received as he grew more educated; and the huge impact he made on Torah study, an impact felt to this day among Jewish students of Torah and Talmud. (The Talmud is the greatly revered, vast body of commentaries on the Torah [written law], plus what is called the oral law.) It was said that Rabbi Akiva "did for the oral law what Ezra had done for the written law."[2]

HIS HUMBLE BEGINNINGS

Akiva belonged to the *am ha'aretz* (people of the land), not to the priestly tribe of Levi or the high priestly line. In fact, he was either the son or grandson of a Gentile convert.[3] He had no formal education and earned his living by shepherding sheep. Yet Akiva's lack of education was not a problem to him. Rather, he had little regard for the highly educated, saying, "Had I a scholar in my power I would maul him."[4] Akiva was an unlikely candidate to become a Torah scholar.

HIS HELPER

Akiva worked for a wealthy landowner named Ben Kalba Savua. For some reason, Rachel, the landowner's daughter, saw Akiva's potential to become a great Torah scholar. One day she approached him with a proposition of marriage. Attached to it, however, was a condition. They would marry only if he would begin to study the Torah as soon as possible. Though caught off guard by the offer, the forty-year-old Akiva was intrigued. Rachel did not know Akiva's disdain for scholars. As he pondered the proposal, he came across a natural pool containing a hollowed-out rock that rested on a waterfall. He began to reason, "If water, which is soft, can hollow out a stone, which is hard, how much more will the words of the Torah, which are hard, cut through and make an impression on my heart, which is soft."[5]

The couple married despite opposition from Rachel's father, who opposed the union because of Akiva's low station in life. Ben Kalba Savua disowned both of them. Although undertaking intense Torah study was a Herculean task, Akiva began his quest by mastering the Hebrew alphabet. Slowly, yet thoroughly, his knowledge grew. Rachel was a constant, daily encouragement to him. Though life was difficult, she did all she could to help support the family, including selling her hair to bring in money. Eventually Akiva had to leave home to study under prominent rabbis. Rachel knew the importance of such a move and encouraged and persuaded him to go. He returned twelve years later as an ordained rabbi, the head of his own yeshiva (Jewish school), with twelve thousand students.[6]

The story is told that, as he returned home, he heard Rachel tell a neighbor she would "willingly wait another twelve years for Akiva to increase his learning twofold. He left immediately for another twelve years, not even showing himself to her."[7] When he returned the second time (a twenty-four year total), she ran to him and "prostrated herself at his feet. When his students moved to push her away, he restrained them saying, 'All the Torah knowledge that I have, and all the Torah knowledge that you have, are the direct results of this woman's love of the Torah.'"[8] Akiva was acutely aware that his position as a great rabbi was only a reality because of the sacrifice and support of his wife, Rachel.

HIS IMPACT

Tannaim were learned men who interpreted and explained Torah and Talmud. According to Jewish tradition, God gave an oral, as well as written, law to Moses on Mt. Sinai. (Scripture does not support this position.) Over the years, many scholars have considered Akiva the greatest of the *tannaim* because he organized the *Halacha* (law) in an outline form. He drew up the six major divisions or areas that would be used as the template for Judah Ha-Nisi, the last of the *tannaim*, as the basis for what is known today as the Mishna.[9]

Akiva lived when Rome controlled Israel. Most of that time, the atmosphere was not conducive to Torah study. Many difficult years culminated in the destruction of the Temple in A.D. 70. By the time Hadrian became emperor, the Temple had been in ruins for fifty years. Hadrian's rise to power brought temporary hope because, early in his rule, he desired to win the trust of his subjects. But hope died when he came to believe the Jewish people were not trustworthy; and he decreed it illegal to read and study Torah, as well as to observe the Sabbath. These "crimes" were punishable by death.

Persecution increased, and thousands of rabbis died. Asked by one of his students why he continued to teach and study

Torah, Akiva replied in the form of a story:

> To what is the matter like? To a fox who was walking
> along the banks of a stream, and saw some fishes gath-
> ering together to move from one place to another. He
> said to them, "From what are you fleeing?" They
> answered: "From the nets which men are bringing
> against us." He said to them: "Let it be your pleasure
> to come on dry land, and let us, I and you, dwell
> together, even as my fathers dwelt with your fathers."
> They replied: "Are you the animal who they say is the
> shrewdest of animals? You are not clever, but a fool!
> For if we are afraid in this place which is our life-ele-
> ment, how much more so in a place which is our death-
> element!" So also is it with us: If now, while we sit and
> study Torah, in which it is written, "For this is your
> life and the length of your days"(Dt. 30:20), we are in
> such a plight, how much more so if we neglect it?[10]

Rabbi Akiva possessed a unique capacity to laugh in the face
of terrible circumstances. When the Roman legions were advanc-
ing toward them, the sages asked him why he was laughing:

> "Idol worshipers dwell in peace and security, while
> the holy Temple is burnt to the ground . . . shall we
> not cry?"
>
> "That's why I'm laughing," said Rabbi Akiva. "If
> this is how G-d rewards the Romans—who are so
> wicked and cruel—for the good deeds they sometimes
> do, how much more will be the reward of the righteous
> people in the World to come."[11]

As the noose of Roman persecution tightened around the
Jewish people, Hadrian ordered the ruins of Jerusalem rebuilt
and dedicated to the Roman god Jupiter. A now very old Rabbi
Akiva encouraged a revolt. Quoting from Numbers 24:17
("There shall come a Star out of Jacob, and a Scepter shall rise out
of Israel, and shall smite the corners of Moab, and destroy all the

children of Sheth"), Akiva pronounced Simon bar Koseba, known for his strength and courage, as messiah. Bar Koseba became known as Simon Bar Kochba (son of a star).

At first Bar Kochba seemed successful, but the rebellion soon turned to disaster. More than 500,000 Jewish people were killed and one thousand villages destroyed. Jerusalem was rebuilt—not by the Jews, for the Jews—but by the Romans as a Roman city called Aelia Capitolina. It was then that Israel began to be called "Palestina," a practice still used today.

Rabbi Akiva, in his eighties, was captured and flayed alive. Even as he was tortured, he reportedly laughed:

> All my life I've been waiting to fulfill the concept "You shall love Hashem [literally, "the name"; a reference to the Lord] your G-d, with all your heart and with all your soul . . . " and now I finally have the chance.[12]

Rabbi Akiva holds a place of greatness among the Jewish people because he was "great in Torah, great in love of Hashem, great in 'Emunah,' 'Belief,' in the Almighty, and great in appreciation of and devotion to his wife."[13]

As Christians, we don't recognize oral law as inspired from God. Yet Christian Bible students have sometimes gained fresh insights to Old Testament texts through Rabbi Akiva's commentary.

His quest to know Torah, begun at age forty, demonstrates that one is never too old to begin studying the Word. And his faithful Rachel demonstrates the importance of a wife who believes in her husband.

But most important, Rabbi Akiva's life also demonstrates that intelligence, sincerity, and dedication are not the ingredients required to identify the Messiah of Israel. Reading God's Word, trusting in the plain meaning of Scripture, and believing it are the essentials. Rabbi Akiva looked to a false messiah because he allowed the terrible conditions of his day to cloud his thinking. Eternity and our place in it hang in the balance; therefore, it is crucial we look to the truth.

WANTING TO BE A SOMEBODY

WRITTEN IN THE FLYLEAF OF ONE OF MY books are the words, *Great to be a somebody. I'm most grateful for everything. T. G.* [Thank God]. A friend of mine wrote those words in 1960. When he wrote that note, Max was indeed a "somebody." An immigrant child whose roots were out of the Pale, he had the drive and work ethic that propelled him to the kind of success in business that most people only dream of.

An avid reader, Max bought books—usually about Judaism—and made notations on the end pages about key events in his life. Sometimes the notes were written like prayers to God. His library and recorded history grew.

By the time I met Max, the words he wrote in 1960 had become ancient history. The Max I met was a surviving stroke patient and a pauper, having lost his shoe business and all of the trappings of his success. He had gone from being a somebody to being a nobody. But he still had the drive and zeal for life that exemplified immigrants or children of immigrants from the Pale.

John Adams, the second president of the United States, said, "The Hebrews have done more to civilize man than any other nation." He said that even if he were an atheist, he would believe that fate ordained the Jews to be the "most essential instrument for civilizing the nations." Following are a few examples of immigrants and their children from the Pale of Settlement who epitomized Adams' statement and impacted the world.

Irving Berlin: Born the son of a cantor in 1888, Israel Baline came to America from Siberia at the age of four. His name was changed to Irving Berlin, and he grew up in New York with no musical training. Yet for more than fifty years he brought to the world a style of music that enriched generations. "White Christmas," "Easter Parade," and "God Bless America" are but three of the favorites.

Eddie Cantor: Born Isidor Iskowitch, he was raised on the Lower East Side of New York in extreme poverty. In addition to his accomplishments as a performer, Cantor founded the March of Dimes. He was awarded an honorary doctoral degree in Humane Letters from Temple University, as well as a medal by President Lyndon Johnson for services rendered to his country and the world.

Casimir Funk: Funk came to the United States in 1915 from his native Poland. By that time he had already received a Ph.D. in chemistry. Funk discovered a cure for beriberi. He identified the curative substance as an amine and proposed that it be called *vitamine* for *vital amine*. Casimir Funk and a British colleague were able to discern that many physical conditions were caused by a vitamin-deficient diet.

Shmuel Gelbfise (better known as **Samuel Goldwyn**): Born in Warsaw in 1882, Goldwyn came to America at the age of thirteen. Starting out as a glove salesman, he worked his way up to become the owner of a glove factory. Goldwyn left that successful enterprise to pioneer a work in motion pictures, and for more than thirty-five years he made what many regarded as the finest movies. He used his profits, which ran into the millions of dollars, to fund the Samuel Goldwyn Foundation, a charity that assisted philanthropic causes. The "G" in MGM Studios stands for Goldwyn.

Dr. Joseph Goldberger: Migrating from the Pale, Goldberger did extensive research in the study of infectious diseases. His research led to the elimination of pellagra, an intestinal disorder brought about by a niacin deficiency.

Al Jolson: Ase Yoelson was born in Saint Petersburg, Russia, in 1886, the son of a cantor. Coming to the United States at the age of seven altered his family's plans for him. He had no interest, as had the five previous generations, in singing for the synagogue. His desire was to entertain people. His career on the stage, in vaudeville, on radio, and in the movies propelled him to become one of the most popular singers of his time. (My father still loves him!) When he died in 1950, more than twenty thousand mourners attended his funeral.

Anna Rosenberg: Born in Budapest in 1902, Anna came to America in 1912. After serving in labor relations, she became a consultant to mayors, governors, and presidents. She went on to become the first female U.S. assistant secretary of defense, under George Marshall. In addition, she received the Medal of Merit, the first woman to be so honored.

David Sarnoff: Born in 1891 in Russia, Sarnoff was nine years old when he came to the United States. His interest in electronics led him to work as the operator of the telegraph station for John Wanamaker's department store in New York. On the evening of April 14, 1912, it was Sarnoff who received the distress call of the SS *Titanic*. In 1926, as general manager of RCA, Sarnoff created NBC (National Broadcasting Company) as a subsidiary of RCA. He retired as chairman of RCA in 1970. Some of the first events he brought into the homes of Americans included major league baseball and football.

Selman Abraham Waksman: Born in Priluka, Russia, in 1888, he immigrated to America in 1910 and became one of the world's foremost authorities on soil microbiology. Waksman discovered the antibiotic streptomycin, the first effective medicine to control and treat tuberculosis. This discovery earned him the Nobel Prize for medicine in 1953. Defying the stereotype, he signed his rights to the earnings from his discovery over to Rutgers University, where he served as head of the Institute of Microbiology.

These are but a few of the accomplished Jewish immigrants whose roots were in the Pale—perhaps like some of your own acquaintances. Like my friend Max, they had the interest, drive, and zeal it took to become "somebodies."

In the days of his financial success, two of Max's employees shared Jesus, the Messiah and Savior, with him. They kept in contact with him after he became ill and his business failed. By the time I met Max, through these two faithful believers he had trusted Christ and was completely unashamed of his new relationship with Him. Most of his family members thought this change was a result of the stroke, when, in fact, his mind was as sharp as a tack. He always wanted me to visit him to read the Bible or share Christ with a family member. Because of Max, I got to know most of his family and we became good friends. When Max died, his daughter called and offered me any books I might want from his library. He wanted me to have them. I feel privileged to own, not only his old books, but all of the notations in them.

When Max wrote the words in his book in 1960, he thought he was a somebody, when, in truth, he was going nowhere. In old age and death, Max had become a nobody in the eyes of the world. To God, however, he was a *SOMEBODY* through His Son, Jesus Christ.

PLAY BALL!

SPORTS RADIO, A RELATIVE NEWCOMER in the arena known as talk radio, is a result of the mutual admiration between professional athletes and the fans who watch them.

The last names of the people who produce, direct, and host many of these programs read like the membership list of a typical synagogue. Add in the people who frequently call these shows, and you can quickly see that many Jewish people are passionate about sports. In fact, Jewish people around the world love all kinds of sports; their fervor is not limited.

In Israel, soccer and basketball are extremely popular, with fans filling arenas and watching regularly on television. Canada's Jewish population has an avid love for hockey. In New York City, home of the largest Jewish population in the world outside Israel, fans speak of their sports teams with the same passion as yeshiva students debating the Talmud.

Yet, according to traditional Judaism, this zeal for sports should never have arisen. Dating back to the time of Hellenism (323–330 B.C.)[1], Jewish leaders taught that involvement in sports was pagan. In those days, athletes participated in the nude. The practice was considered unclean, a violation of both rabbinic teaching and Hebrew Scripture.

Jewish people knew that to practice paganism was considered rebellion against God. Rather, they were to pursue separated, sanctified living. In addition, with little free time available, athletics were considered wasteful. Therefore, it was felt that time would be better spent studying and learning, rather than becoming polluted by the world. Through the years, this emphasis has resulted in a people much better known for producing doctors, lawyers, teachers, and social workers than athletes who could hit home runs, score touchdowns, sink baskets, or score goals.

Around two thousand years later, the Holocaust dramatically changed the Jewish community of Europe, and millions of Jewish people bravely made the move from the Old World to America.

Over time Jewish families in America became less observant in their faith than they were in Europe. Their strong work ethic, allowed to flourish in a country blessed with freedom, eventually afforded them access to a lifestyle with increased leisure time. And their free environment provided accessibility to the national culture, which exposed them to new interests.

Consequently, there arose a new generation of Jewish people who began to transfer to sports the zeal their parents and grandparents had applied to religion. The scenario was mirrored in almost every free country where Jewish people found themselves.

On October 6, 1965, Jewishness and professional athletics collided in a way that profoundly affected the Jewish community. If you ask Jewish people born in the 1950s or earlier what happened that day, and you remind them that it was Yom Kippur (Day of Atonement), the highest holy day on the Jewish calendar, you might see a grin spread across their faces.

I remember that date well. Like most Jewish people, I spent the entire day with my family in *shul* (Yiddish for "synagogue"). Between liturgies, there was much talk that had nothing to do with atonement. It centered, of all things, on baseball.

The World Series had started that afternoon between the Minnesota Twins and Los Angeles Dodgers. It was the opening game, the most important in the seven-game series of a sport that was arguably the most popular one in America at the time. The identity of the teams was of little or no concern to our Cleveland, Ohio, congregation. Even the fact that one of the teams had a Jewish pitcher was not sufficient motivation to talk during the service.

What generated the enormous buzz in our synagogue that day was the fact that the Dodgers' Jewish pitcher, Sandy Koufax, had made a decision that rocked the news media and spread like wildfire across the nation's newspapers and airwaves. Koufax had refused to pitch the first game of the Series because it fell on Yom Kippur.

His reason was simple: He was Jewish. Just how big was that personal decision? Big enough that it had the entire Jewish community in the United States talking. And big enough to become a subject that Jewish people still discuss today.

In her book *Sandy Koufax* (HarperCollins), published in 2002, Jane Leavy put it this way:

> *By refusing to pitch, Koufax defined himself as a man of principle who placed faith above craft. He became inextricably linked with the American Jewish experience. . . . In Jewish households, he was the New Patriarch: Abraham, Isaac, Jacob, and Sandee.*[2]

His decision enshrined him forever in Jewish hearts; and Koufax, now 67, is spoken of fondly to this day:

> *You see him on the menu at Gallagher's Steak House in New York, on the wall mural celebrating the history of the Jews outside Cantor's deli in Los Angeles, . . . on the library shelves at the Washington Hebrew Congregation in Washington, D.C. The [his] paperback biography, a quickie clip job published in 1968, was so well thumbed librarians had to put it between*

hard covers. It remains the most asked for book in the synagogue's children's collection.[3]

Sandy Koufax was not an observant Jew; but Rabbi Hillel Silverman, whom Ms. Leavy said "annually invoked Koufax's name in his Yom Kippur sermon," provided Koufax's reasoning. Rabbi Silverman said Koufax told him, "I'm Jewish. I'm a role model. I want them to understand they have to have pride."[4] The rabbi told his congregants, "Not being observant and feeling a connection with his people, it's [Koufax's refusal to pitch] an even greater sacrifice."[5]

Although he might be the best known of Jewish athletes, Sandy Koufax is not the only one. In fact, quite a number of them "rebelled" and found their place in the world of sports. The following list is by no means exhaustive, but rather provides a few names of Jewish people who have contributed significantly to the field of sports.

BASEBALL

Few people realize that Lipman Pike was "the first Jewish major leaguer" and "baseball's first undisputed homerun king"[6] or that Ron Bloomberg was the first designated hitter. Yet many are familiar with the names of infielder Al Rosen; outfielders Hank Greenberg, Shawn Green, and Gabe Kapler; and pitchers Steve Stone and Ken Holtzman. Jewish Americans have long been enamored with the game of baseball.

BASKETBALL

Eddie Gottlieb may not be the name on everyone's tongue; but the fact is, Gottlieb was a founder of the National Basketball Association (NBA), a successful coach and basketball mogul, and a member of the Basketball Hall of Fame.

One of the most successful basketball coaches, winning nine NBA titles and called the "4th winningest coach" in NBA history, is Arnold (Red) Auerbach—also the Boston Celtics' successful general manager and president. William (Red) Holzman was the

Hall of Famer who led the New York Knicks to their only two NBA championships and 613 victories.[7] Wrote Robert Slater: "He compiled a better record than any other active coach in pro basketball."[8] Larry Brown, a former American Basketball Association player, is known for his superb coaching in both college and professional basketball.

Ernie Grunfield, a former NBA player, served as general manager of the New York Knicks and currently serves in the same position for the Milwaukee Bucks. Adolph and his son Dan Shayes both played in the NBA. Abraham "Abe" Saperstein founded the world famous Harlem Globetrotters. And the current NBA commissioner is David Stern.

OLYMPICS

Many people know the name Mark Spitz, considered by some to be the greatest Jewish athlete of all time. In the 1972 Olympics, Spitz swam his way to a record seven gold medals.

And who can forget 18-year-old Kerri Strug, who in 1996 bravely vaulted the U.S. Women's Gymnastics Team to its first gold medal in history despite a broken ankle? The late Charlotte "Eppy" Epstein is considered "the mother of American women's swimming."[9] She led the first women's team in the Olympics in 1920. Harold Abrahams became better known as people viewed the Academy Award-winning movie *Chariots of Fire*. Abrahams won the Olympic gold for England in the 100-meter dash in 1924.

Yael Arad became the first Israeli to win an Olympic medal, winning the silver medal in judo in the Barcelona Olympics in 1992. Jewish athlete Margareth Nergman never made it to the Olympics because the Nazis forced her off the German team in 1936. She excelled in fencing and the high jump.

FOOTBALL

There have been but a few Jewish American football players. Ron Mix, a Hall of Famer, played the obscure position of offensive lineman, while Randy Grossman was a less successful tight end. Current quarterback for the Miami Dolphins, Jay Fielder, is trying to follow in the footsteps of Sid Luckman, who led the Chicago Bears to four titles and was named the NFL's most valuable player three times. Marv Levy coached the Buffalo Bills to four Super Bowls. Owners of NFL teams include the late Leon Hess of the New York Jets; current owner of the Oakland Raiders, Al Davis; and the New York Mets' Fred Wilpon.

OTHERS

Several Jewish people have been successful at tennis, including Angela Buxton who won the Wimbledon doubles championship in 1956 and became the world's fifth ranked women's player that year. Highly ranked Brian Gottfried played in the '70s and '80s, and Brad Gilbert plays now.

It would be remiss not to mention the names of several Jewish men who left their mark as sports announcers. These include the late greats Howard Cosell, Mel Allen, and Marty Glickman. When Glickman was eighteen, the Nazis barred him from competing in the 1936 Berlin Olympics as a sprinter because he was Jewish.

The Jewish love for athletics, coupled with the success of various Jewish athletes, resulted in the founding of the Jewish Sports Hall of Fame in 1979 in Netanya, Israel, not far from Tel Aviv.[10] Those honored are distinguished athletes who are recognized for their extraordinary abilities.

Unfortunately, the world loves stereotypes. It projects an image of Jewish people as financiers, doctors, and lawyers. Certainly many Jewish people hold positions that require much education, partly because education is one thing persecution cannot take away from you. But they have left their mark in other areas as well, and their accomplishments in sports have blessed millions around the world.

ENDNOTES

PIONEERING SPIRIT—PAGES 15–19
[1] Irving Howe and Kenneth Libo, *How We Lived* (New York: Richard Marek Publishers, Inc., 1979), 26.
[2] Ibid., Morris Rosenfeld, 157.

RETURNING TO THE LAND—PAGES 21–26
[1] Paul J. Deegan, *The Kibbutz, Life on an Israeli Commune* (Mankato, MN: Amecus Street Book, 1971), 8.
[2] Rabbi Joseph Telushkin, *Jewish Literacy* (New York: William Morrow and Company, Inc., 1991), 272.
[3] *Encyclopaedia Judaica* CD-Rom Edition, s. v. "Jewish National Fund" and "Keren Kayemet le-Israel."
[4] "Kibbutz, What Is It?" About Kibbutz [www.oranim.macam98.ac.il/kibbutz/about.htm], Oren Kibbutz Institutes for Jewish Experience [www.oranim.macam98.ac.il/kibbutz/kibbutz.html].

LOST HOPE RECLAIMED—PAGES 27–32
[1] J. Vernon McGee, *Psalms* (California: Thru The Bible Books, 1982), 3:149–50.
[2] Bathja Bayer, "Ha-tikva," *Encyclopaedia Judaica* CD-Rom Edition.
[3] "How 'Hatikvah' Became Israel's National Anthem by Default," Carl Schrag, *Jerusalem Post Service*, June 5, 1998, cited by Jewish Bulletin of Northern California Online, [www.jewishf.com/bk980605/supphow.htm], [www.jewish.com/current/jbfooter.map?50, 9].

THE MAN WHO BROUGHT HEBREW BACK TO THE LAND—PAGES 33–38
[1] "The History of Eliezer Ben-Yehuda Hebrew" [www.levsoftware.com/history/htm].
[2] Ibid.
[3] Ibid.
[4] Rabbi Barry Freundel, "For the Sake of Jerusalem, Be Silent . . . Sometimes" [www.kesher.org/r_jerusa.htm].
[5] "The History of Eliezer Ben-Yehuda Hebrew."
[6] "Ben-Yehuda, Eliezer (1858–1922)" [www.jajzed.org.il/100/people/bios/beliezer.html].

THE FIRST LINE OF DEFENSE—PAGES 39–45
[1] Dennis Eisenberg, Uri Dan, Eli Landau, *The Mossad, Israel's Secret Intelligence Service Inside Stories* (New York: Signet Book, 1978), 256.
[2] Benjamin Netanyahu, *A Place Among the Nations* (New York: Bantam, 1993), xiii.
[3] Eisenberg, 27.
[4] Ibid., 30.

ARE THERE HORNS UNDER THAT HAT?—PAGES 47–53
[1] David A. Rausch, *A Legacy of Hatred* (Chicago: Moody Press, 1984), 22.
[2] Deborah Lipstadt, *Denying the Holocaust* (New York: The Free Press, 1993), 9.
[3] Ibid., 99.
[4] Ibid., 53.

[5] Ibid., 23.

[6] Ibid., 63.

[7] Rausch, 130.

[8] Bryon L. Sherwin and Susan G. Ament, *Encountering the Holocaust* (Chicago: Impact Press, 1979), 22.

[9] Lipstadt, 225.

IS THE NEW TESTAMENT ANTI-SEMITIC?—PAGES 55–61

[1] Cited by Paul L. Maier in "Who Killed Jesus" [www.christianitytoday.com/ct/2000/134/42.0.html], August 24, 2000.

[2] Ben Birnbaum, "A Legacy of Blood," *Moment Magazine*, October 2001, 88.

[3] Maier.

[4] Ibid.

[5] Birnbaum, 50.

[6] Skip Bayless, "Context Factor in How to View Ward's Words," *Chicago Tribune* [http://chicagosports.com/columnists/content/column/0%2C2007%2C150203%2C00.html], April 25, 2001.

[7] "A Legacy of Hate: The Long War Against Israel," audio tape #1 of 2, (Spring Valley, Calif.: Family Tape Ministry).

[8] David Cooper, *The Messianic Series: The God of Israel* (Los Angeles, Calif.: Biblical Research Society, 1967), first page.

[9] Birnbaum, 91.

[10] Ibid., 55.

[11] Phil Jasner, "Chaplain Surprised by Knick Comments," *Philadelphia Daily News*, April 23, 2001, 2.

[12] Al Brickner, "The Jewishness of the New Testament" [www.yashanet.com/library/brickner.htm].

JEWISH HUMOR—PAGES 67–72

[1] *Encyclopaedia Judaica* CD-Rom Edition, s. v. "Jewish Humor."

[2] William Novak and Moshe Waldoks, eds., *The Big Book of Jewish Humor* (New York: Harper Perennial, 1990), 4–5.

[3] Ibid., 44.

[4] Leslie B. Flynn, *What the Church Owes the Jew* (n.p.: Magnus Press, 1998), 90.

[5] *Encyclopaedia Judaica* CD-Rom Edition, s. v. "Shalom Aleichem."

[6] Sarah Silberstein Swartz, *Bar Mitzvah* (New York: Doubleday, 1985), 50.

JEWISH MUSIC—PAGES 73–83

[1] *Encyclopaedia Judaica* CD-Rom Edition, s. v. "Music."

[2] "Music," P. J. Achtemeier *Harper's Bible Dictionary* (San Francisco: Harper & Row, 1985), 669 (published in electronic form by Logos Research Systems, 1996).

[3] *The New Scofield Study Bible* (New York: Oxford University Press, 1967), 664 n.

[4] Charles Ryrie, "Introduction to the Book of Psalms," *Ryrie Study Bible* (Chicago: Moody Press, 1976), 798.

[5] Ibid.

[6] Achtemeier, 667.

[7] Ibid., 671.

[8] Abraham E. Millgram, *Jewish Worship* (Philadelphia: The Jewish Publication Society of America, 1971), 364.

9 "Jewish Music" [www.templesanjose.org/JudaismInfo/song/music.htm].
10 Rabbi Hayim Halevy Donin, *To Pray As a Jew* (New York: Basic Books, Inc., 1980), 21.
11 Ibid.
12 "Jewish Music."
13 Ibid.
14 Millgram, 365.
15 Ibid., 366.
16 Richard Siegel and Carl Rheins, eds., *The Jewish Almanac* (New York: Bantam Books, 1980), 462.
17 Ibid., 468.
18 "Jewish Music."
19 Ari Davidow, "About the Klezmer Revival" [www.well.com/user/ari/klez/articles/aboutklez.html].
20 Larry Maxey, "Klezmer and the Klarinette" [www.clarinet.org/Research/2000/Maxey.htm].
21 Ibid.
22 Moshe Denburg, "Jewish Music—An Overview" [www.us-Israel.org/jsource/Judaism/music.html].

FROM BADGE TO BANNER—PAGES 85–88
1 *Encyclopaedia Judaica* CD-Rom Edition, s. v. "Flag."
2 "The Israeli Flag," "How the Israeli Flag Was Chosen?" [www.us-israel.org/jsource/History/isflag.html].
3 *Encyclopaedia Judaica.*
4 "The Israeli Flag," "The Magen David" [www.us-israel.org.jsource/History/isflag.html].

WHAT'S IN A NAME?—PAGES 101–104
1 Dan Rottenburg, *Finding Our Fathers* (New York: Random House, 1977), 48.

SO, WHAT EXACTLY IS THAT?—PAGES 105–109
1 Rabbi Yaakov Kleiman, "The Cohanim/DNA Connection" [aish.com/societywork/sciencenature/].
2 Philip Birnbaum, "rabbinate," *Encyclopedia of Jewish Concepts* (New York: Hebrew Publishing Company, 1995), 565.
3 Rabbi Joseph Telushkin, "Rabbinic Ordination/Semikha," *Jewish Literacy* (New York: William Morrow & Company, Inc., 1991), 646–7.
4 Ibid.
5 "Rabbis, Priests and Other Religious Functionaries" [www.jewfaq.org].

A DAY FOR REMEMBERING YOM HASHOAH—PAGES 111–116
1 General fundraising letter of the U.S. Holocaust Memorial Museum, undated.
2 Ibid.
3 Jennifer Rosenberg, "Holocaust Remembrance Day" [http://history1900s.about.com/library/holocaust/aa042398.htm].
4 Ibid.
5 Rabbi Yehuda Prero, "Yom HaShoah—How to Remember the Holocaust" [www.torah.org/learning/yomtov/holocaust/no1.html].

[6] *The Jerusalem Post Internet Edition*, "News From Israel," August 30, 2001, [www.jpost.com/Editions/2001/08/30/News/News.33743.html].

[7] Jimmy DeYoung, *Prophecy Today*, September 4, 2001, [www.gospelcom.net/shofar/pp/html/article.php].

THE CALL OF THE SHOFAR—PAGES 117–121
[1] Alfred J. Kolatch, *The Jewish Book of Why* (Middle Village, NY: Jonathan David Publishers, 1981), 224–225.

GIVING AND RECEIVING THE BLESSING—PAGES 123–126
[1] *Encyclopaedia Judaica* CD-Rom Edition, s. v. "Priestly Blessing."

ALIYAH FOR THE PEOPLE OF THE BOOK—PAGES 127–132
[1] Judaic Collection Tree of Life Bookmark (Lawrenceville, N.J.: Lenox, Incorporated), 1.
[2] *Encyclopaedia Judaica*, s. v. "Torah."

BLESSINGS ON YOUR HEAD—PAGES 133–138
[1] "Prayers and Blessings" [www.jewfaq.org/prayer.htm].
[2] *Encyclopaedia Judaica* CD-Rom Edition, s. v. "Benedictions."
[3] Philip Birnbaum, *The Book of Jewish Concepts* (New York: Hebrew Publishing Company, 1964), 98.
[4] Ibid.
[5] Alfred J. Kolatch, *The Second Jewish Book of Why* (Middle Village, N.Y.: Jonathan David Publishers, Inc., 1985), 235.
[6] *Encyclopaedia Judaica* CD-Rom Edition, s. v. "Grace after Meals."
[7] *Encyclopaedia Judaica* CD-Rom Edition, s. v. "Laws of Benedictions."
[8] Rabbi Adin Steinsaltz, *A Guide to Jewish Prayer* (New York: Schocken Books, 2000), 8.
[9] Birnbaum, 292.
[10] "Ask the Rabbi," "Kippah Athletics," "The Aish Rabbi Replies" [www.aish.com/rabbi/ATR_browse.asp?s=kippah&f=tqak&offset=1].

JUDAISM VS. JEWISHNESS—PAGES 139–143
[1] *Jewish Exponent*, July 29, 1999, 21.
[2] Milton Steinberg, *Basic Judaism* (San Diego: Harvest/HBJ, 1975), 3.
[3] Joseph L. Blau, *Modern Varieties of Judaism* (New York: Columbia University Press, 1966), 160.
[4] R. Albert Mohler Jr., *World*, Sept. 25, 1999, 21.

CHOSEN? FOR WHAT?—PAGES 145–150
[1] Harold P. Smith, *A Treasure Hunt in Judaism* (New York: Hebrew Publishing Company, 1950), 122.
[2] Marc H. Tanenbaum, Marvin R. Wilson, and A. James Ruden, eds., *Evangelicals and Jews in Conversation on Scripture, Theology, and History* (Grand Rapids: Baker Book House, 1978), 19.
[3] Alfred J. Kolatch, *The Second Jewish Book of Why* (Middle Village, N.Y.: Jonathan David Publishers, Inc., 1985), 23.
[4] Herman Wouk, *This Is My God* (Garden City, N.J.: Doubleday & Co., Inc., 1959), 33.

[5] Kolatch, 22–23.

[6] Philip Birnbaum, *The Book of Jewish Concepts* (New York: Hebrew Publishing Company, 1964), 70–71.

[7] *Encyclopaedia Britannica*, 1999–2000 Britannica.com Inc., s. v. "Chosen People."

[8] Steven S. Schwarzchild, "Noachide Laws," *Encyclopaedia Judaica* CD-Rom Edition.

[9] Rabbi Joseph Telushkin, *Jewish Literacy* (New York: William Morrow and Company, Inc.), 509.

[10] Ibid., 506.

WHEN YOU'RE DEAD, YOU'RE DEAD—PAGES 151–156

[1] Rifat Sonsino and Daniel B Syme, *What Happens After I Die? Jewish Views of Life After Death* (New York: UAHC Press), 8.

[2] Ibid., 56.

[3] Ibid., 57.

[4] Ibid., 59.

[5] Arthur A. Cohen, *Contemporary Jewish Religious Thought Resurrection of the Dead* (New York: Charles Scribner's Sons, 1987), 807.

[6] Geoffrey Wigoder, ed., *Encyclopedia of Judaism* (New York: Macmillan Publishers, 1997), 37.

[7] Sonsino and Syme, 46.

[8] "Olam Ha-Ba: The Afterlife" [www.jewfaq.org/olamhaba.htm].

[9] Sonsino and Syme, 29.

[10] Ibid.

[11] Class notes, Yeshiva Ha-Dat, 1963.

[12] Sonsino and Syme, 26.

[13] Class notes.

[14] "Olam Ha-Ba: The Afterlife."

PONDERING THE QUESTION OF EVIL—PAGES 157–162

[1] Eugene B. Borowitz, *Understanding Judaism* (New York: Union of American Hebrew Congregations, 1979), 7.

[2] Ibid., 8.

[3] Rabbi Morris Silverman, ed., *Passover Haggadah* (Connecticut: Prayer Book Press, 1959), x.

[4] "Human Nature," "The Dual Nature" [www.jewfaq.org/human.htm].

[5] Borowitz, 9.

[6] Rabbi Yechiel Eckstein, *What Christians Should Know About Jews and Judaism* (Texas: Word Books, 1984), 67.

[7] Jacob J. Petuchowski, *Our Masters Taught: Rabbinic Stories and Sayings* (New York: The Crossroad Publishing Company, 1982), 21.

[8] *Encyclopaedia Judaica* CD-ROM Edition, s. v. "Good and Evil" "In Talmudic Literature,"

[9] "Human Nature."

TIKKUN OLAM—PAGES 163–168

[1] Dr. A. TH. Philips, *Daily Prayers* (New York: Hebrew Publishing Company, n.d.), 149–150.

[2] *Encyclopaedia Judaica* CD-Rom Edition, s. v. "aleinu le-shabbe'ah."

[3] Joseph Naft, "Tikkun Olam: Perfecting the World" [www.innerfrontier.org/Practices/TikkunOlam.htm].

[4] Francine Klagsbrun, "Repairing the World" [www.momentmag.com/columnists/index1.html].

[5] Ibid.

[6] "Jewish Ethics," "Tikkun Olam" [www.mishpacha. com/tzedakah.shtml].

[7] Zalman Myersmith, "Letter from America" [www.newwestend.org.uk/magP02/America.htm].

[8] Rabbi Margaret Holub, "Tikkun," "Rabbi's Notes–November 2001" [www.mcjc.org/mjoldart/MJAMH033.htm].

[9] Jack Newfield, "An interview with Mario Cuomo," interview by Jack Newfield [www.findarticles.com/m1548/n3_v13/20925642/p1/article.jhtml], May-June 1998.

[10] "Senator Joe Lieberman: In Praise of 'Tikkun Olam'" [www.jewishpost.com/jp0610/jpn0610h.htm].

[11] Holub.

THE TATOO IS TABOO—PAGES 169–172

[1] Alfred J. Kolatch, *The Second Jewish Book of Why* (Middle Village, N.Y.: Jonathan David Publishers, Inc., 1985), 171.

[2] Ibid., 31a, 21.

[3] *To Be a Jew*, 180, quoting Shabbat 156b.

ORGANIZED FOR SERVICE—PAGES 173–178

[1] *Encyclopaedia Judaica*, s. v. "B'nai Brith."

[2] "B'nai B'rith International: A Record of Innovation" [www.bnaibrith.org/whatis/history.html].

[3] *Encyclopaedia Judaica*.

[4] Deborah Pessin, *History of Jews in America* (New York, N.Y.: United Synagogue of America, 1957), 128.

[5] "B'nai B'rith International: A Record of Innovation."

[6] Ibid.

[7] Ibid.

[8] Pessin, 128.

[9] "Milestones in the History of Ort" [www.aort.org].

[10] Ibid.

[11] Ibid.

[12] Dorothy Weinberg, "The Story of Hadassah: From Henrietta Szold to the Woman of the '80s," *Jewish Chicago Magazine*, Hanukkah Issue, 1983.

[13] Ibid.

[14] "Hadassah Today," About Hadassah Medical Organization [www.hadassah.org.il/about/02-today.htm].

[15] Ibid.

[16] *The Jerusalem Report*, October 23, 2000, 23.

WORKMEN'S CIRCLE—PAGES 179–184

[1] Joseph Berger, "Less Socialist but Still Social," *The New York Times*, Metro Edition, October 31, 2002, B6.

[2] Robert Kestenbaum, "Let Social Justice 'Ring'" [www.forward.com/issues/

2002/02.11.08/oped2.html], November 8, 2002.
3 "The Workmen's Circle, Arbeter Ring" [www.circle.org/wccjl.html].
4 *Encyclopaedia Judaica* CD-Rom Edition, s.v. "Workmen's Circle."
5 "The Workmen's Circle, Arbeter Ring."

AKIVA: ASCENSION TO PROMINENCE—PAGES 191–195
1 *Encyclopaedia Judaica*, s.v. "Akiva."
2 Gilbert and Libby Klaperman, *The Story of the Jewish People* (New York: Behrman House, Inc., 1957), 2:155.
3 *Jewish Encyclopedia*, 487.
4 Ibid.
5 Rabbi Joseph Telushkin, *Jewish Literacy* (New York: William Morrow and Company, Inc., 1991), 143.
6 "Elul: A Time to Reflect," "Rabbi Akiva, Master of Teshuvah" [www.ou.org/chagim/elul/akiva.htm].
7 *Jewish Encyclopedia*, 487.
8 "Elul: A Time to Reflect."
9 Klaperman, 174.
10 Telushkin, 143–44.
11 "And Rabbi Akiva Laughed" [www.ohr.org.il/special/9av/3weeks.htm].
12 Ibid.
13 "Elul: A Time to Reflect."

PLAY BALL!—PAGES 201–206
1 *Encyclopaedia Judaica* CD-Rom Edition, s. v. "Hellenism."
2 Jane Leavy, *Sandy Koufax: A Lefty's Legacy* (New York: HarperCollins, 2002), 171.
3 Ibid., xiv.
4 Ibid., 183.
5 Ibid.
6 Peter S. and Joachim Horvitz, *The Big Book of Jewish Baseball*, cited in [www.authorsden.com/visit/viewwork.asp?AuthorID=9386&id=6758].
7 William (Red) Holzman [www.infoplease.com/ipa/ A0771448.html].
8 Robert Slater, *Great Jews in Sports* (Middle Village, N.Y.: Jonathan David Publishers, 1983), 141.
9 Ibid., 70.
10 Ibid., 335.

OTHER MATERIAL FROM STEVE HERZIG

JEWISH CULTURE & CUSTOMS
A Sampler of Jewish Life
Every area of Jewish life radiates with rich symbolism and special meaning. From meals, clothing, and figures of speech to worship, holidays, and weddings, we find hundreds of fascinating traditions that date as far back as two or three thousand years. How did these customs get started? What special meaning do they hold? And what can they teach us? Explore the answers to these questions in this enjoyable sampler of the colorful world of Judaism and Jewish life. You'll gain a greater appreciation for God's Chosen People and see key aspects of the Bible and Christianity in a whole new light.
ISBN 0-915540-31-2, #B68

NOW ON VIDEO—

JEWISH CULTURE & CUSTOMS
A Sampler of Jewish Life
Jewish Culture & Customs is now on video and is a great companion to the book. Filmed on location, this excellent video will delight anyone who wants to understand the Jewish people and the special traditions that have bound them together as an extraordinary nation for thousands of years.
UPC 8-245490-827-3, #V32 (VHS), Approx. 30 minutes

by Elwood McQuaid

THE ZION CONNECTON
Elwood McQuaid takes a thoughtful, sensitive look at relations between Jewish people and evangelical Christians, including the controversial issues of anti-Semitism, the rise of Islam, the right of Jewry to a homeland in the Middle East, and whether Christians should try to reach Jewish people with the gospel message—and how.
ISBN 0-915540-40-1, #B61

ZVI
The Miraculous Story of Triumph Over the Holocaust
For more than half a century, *ZVI* has endured as a best-selling book produced by the ministry of The Friends of Israel. Millions of people have been touched, inspired, and encouraged by this story of a World War II waif in Warsaw, Poland, and how he found his way to Israel and faith in the Messiah to become God's man on the streets of Jerusalem. It is a book you will find difficult to lay down.
ISBN 0-915540-66-5, #B80

IT IS NO DREAM
Said Theodor Herzl, the father of Zionism, "If you will it, it is no dream." This amazing book scans the entire biblical prophetic program and shows how a faithful, promise-keeping God molded historical events to make the modern state of Israel a "dream come true."
ISBN 0-915540-21-5, #B02

by David M. Levy

THE TABERNACLE: SHADOWS OF THE MESSIAH

This best seller on Israel's wilderness Tabernacle explores in depth the service of the priesthood and the significance of the sacrifices. The well-organized content and numerous illustraions will open new vistas of biblical truth as ceremonies, sacrifices, and priestly service reveal the perfections of the Messiah
ISBN 0-915540-17-7, #B51

REVELATION: HEARING THE LAST WORD

Why is there so much uncertainty and disagreement about the last days? What can we know about the Antichrist? In what order will the events of the last days take place? What will happen to Israel during the Tribulation? What will life be like during the Millennial Kingdom? This valuable resource will help you know what we can expect as we approach Earth's final hour
ISBN 0-915540-60-6, #B75

GUARDING THE GOSPEL OF GRACE

We often lack peace, joy, or victory in our walk with Christ because we're not clear how God's grace works in our lives. The books of Galatians and Jude are brought together in this marvelous work that explains grace and what can happen if you stray from it. Don't miss out on the difference that God's grace can make in your life. . . . It's nothing less than amazing!
ISBN 0-915540-26-6, #B67

by Renald E. Showers

MARANATHA: OUR LORD, COME!

A Definitive Study of the Rapture of the Church
Here is an in-depth study of matters related to the Rapture of the church. It addresses such issues as the birth-pang concept in the Bible and ancient Judaism, the biblical concept of the Day of the Lord, the relationship of the Day of the Lord to the Time of Jacob's Trouble and the Great Tribulation, the identification of the sealed scroll of Revelation 5, the significance of the seals, the imminent coming of Christ with His holy angels, the relationship of church saints to the wrath of God, the significance of 2 Thessalonians 2, the implications of both the 70-week prophecy of Daniel 9 and the references to Israel and the church in the book of the Revelation, the meaning of the last trump, and why the timing of the Rapture has practical implications for daily living and ministry.
ISBN 0-915540-22-3 #B55P

THE FOUNDATIONS OF FAITH VOL. ONE

With execptional fidelity to Scripture, Dr. Showers tackles Bibliology and Christology—the doctrines of the Bible and Messiah. Learn what the Bible says about itself, why no other book in the world is like it, the differences between specific and general revelation, what the Bible teaches about Christ, and so much more.
ISBN 0-915540-77-0, #B89 (hardcover)

by Bruce Scott

THE FEASTS OF ISRAEL
Seasons of the Messiah

Many of the Bible's most incredible prophecies about Christ are intricately hidden within the Jewish holidays and feasts of the Old Testament. That's where you'll find little-known yet astounding pictures of Christ's deity, His death and resurrection, and even His Second Coming and future reign as King of kings and Lord of lords. You'll discover that much of what Jesus said and did—which seems mysterious to us today—suddenly makes complete sense. Don't miss any part of the greatest story ever told.
ISBN 0-915540-14-2, #B65

by Lorna Simcox

THE SEARCH

For years Lorna had been on a search for the ultimate truth. You will be enthralled by her true story and the heartwarming journey that finally brought this Jewish woman to faith in her Messiah.
ISBN 0-915540-68-1, #B83

by Victor Buksbazen

ISAIAH'S MESSIAH

From the scholarly pen of Dr. Victor Buksbazen comes an outstanding work on a premier section of the prophetic Hebrew Scriptures, Isaiah 52—53. This superb and attractive little volume masterfully answers the all-important Jewish question, Of whom did the prophet speak? Of Israel, as many rabbis teach, or of Messiah? In an eloquent yet in-depth, verse-by-verse exposition, Dr. Buksbazen shows how Isaiah 53—the only section of the Bible never read in the synagogue—speaks unequivocally of Jesus.

ISBN 0-915540-75-4, #B87 (hardcover)

by Lydia Buksbazen

THEY LOOKED FOR A CITY

You'll hardly be able to lay down this incredible but true story of a Jewish family's bitter but triumphant struggle for survival in Eastern Europe. Travel back to the time of the Russian Cossacks and meet Yente and Benjamin who discover love in the Warsaw Ghetto. How God protected them and enabled them to come to faith is an unforgettable, uplifting story of real-life miracles.

ISBN 0-915540-15-0, #B08

For current prices, to order by credit card, or to obtain a complete catalog of all the resources available from The Friends of Israel, call us at **800-345-8461**; visit our Web store at **www.foi.org**; or write us at **P.O. Box 908, Bellmawr, NJ 08099.**

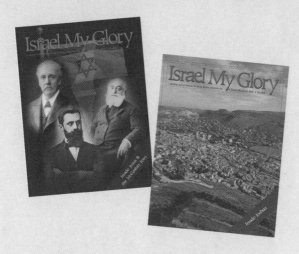